# Hear God's Voice Everyday

### Learn how to hear and recognize the
## Voice of God

# Cindy Edgett

Carpenter's Son Publishing

Hear God's Voice Everyday

Published by Carpenter's Son Publishing, Franklin, Tennessee

Published in association with Larry Carpenter of Christian Book Services, LLC
www.christianbookservices.com

Cover and Interior Design by Adept Content Solutions

Edited by Becky Taylor

Printed in the United States of America

978-1-942587-34-7

To my husband and best friend, Curtis—
Without your love and support, this book would
not have been written. Thank you for encouraging
me every step of the way.

I love you!

Give a man a word from the Lord and he will be edified; teach a man to hear God's voice, and he will have faith that produces hope for a lifetime.

✿   ✿   ✿

**Isaiah 55:3 (NKJV)**
Incline your ear, and come to Me.
Hear, and your soul shall live;
And I will make an everlasting covenant with you—
The sure mercies of David.

# Contents

wk 1

rk 2

# Acknowledgments

To Keith—for teaching me through your life to not keep God in a box because He is so much bigger than that.

To Brandon—for always encouraging me. You have a way of affirming that what I am doing is not only important but is without a doubt from the Lord. Thank you for all of your IT support.

To Reid—for always speaking life into this project and for sharing your excitement with me. Your positive outlook is a constant encouragement.

To Melissa—for teaching me about the heart and mind of young women. God brought you into my life to help prepare me for the girls that would follow you. Thanks for just being you!

To Thayse—Just you being in my life has brought joy and much needed laughter.

To Melissa and Thayse—You have a heart that seeks after the Lord, and a desire to advance the Kingdom of God through your lives. I am so proud of the women you have become! Thanks for prayerfully supporting the process of publishing this book.

Thank you Pastor Ben and Melissa, Debbie, Kathryn, Andrea, Kathy, and Chuck for helping to read and edit this book. Thank you for coming alongside of me in this journey. I am grateful that God has placed each of you in my life.

To Jesus—for helping me to write this book. Your words are an encouragement to me, and I am grateful to have a relationship with You. I love you, Lord!

# Foreword

How do you hear the voice of God? It is a question that humanity has wrestled with for centuries. Does God speak to us? If God does in fact speak, why would He talk to us? And if so, how do we listen, and know with certainty that what we hear is coming from Him?

As a Christian, hearing and knowing God's voice is fundamental to a life-giving relationship with Him. My journey in hearing from God began at age seventeen. I knew that God had clearly spoken to me to go to Bible College, even when others around me did not understand. I moved to Charlotte, North Carolina, with no job, little money, and without tuition, but within just a few weeks, I had a job, a scholarship, and a place to live. Thus began my quest to hear and understand God's voice. All these years later, the sound of His voice is as natural as the voice of the closest of friend's.

As you read this book, you too, can develop an ear for God's voice. This book is based on a solid scriptural foundation that begins at the beginning and plainly demonstrates God's desire for a two-way conversation with us. Personal stories, scripture from the Old and New Testament, as well as practical instruction from personal experience, make this book a go-to manual for hearing and knowing God's voice.

Pastor Ben Pierce
Generation Church

# Introduction

Have you ever met people who say, "God told me this" or "God told me that"? You thought, wow, that seems strange to me that they hear something so clearly and they are so sure of what they heard. Why don't I hear like that? Why does that seem normal for them and not for me? Well, it's because we have not trained ourselves to hear God's voice, to recognize it, or to even be aware of His presence in our lives. Many years ago, I decided that I needed a new normal in my life. This is where it all began for me personally.

I was at a worship practice. We had already practiced the praise and worship set for the weekend. When we had finished practicing, we then began to worship. Some time went by, and there was a sweet presence of the Lord in the room. Everyone was still just lingering in the presence of God. One of the musicians shared this story with the worship team, and it stirred something deep within my spirit. He said that he had been spending time with the Lord, and he realized that he was the one doing all of the talking. So he decided that he was going to stay there until he heard from the Lord. So he grabbed a notebook and pen and just sat there waiting for the Lord to speak. As he sat there, he said that words flooded his mind.

He began writing what he heard. He said at first it seemed like chicken-scratch, but then, it began to flow. The words were coming so fast that he was writing quickly to keep up. Before he knew it, he had written a full page. He set the pen down and re-read what he had written. He said that he was amazed! He said that the Lord really had a lot to tell him; He was just waiting for him to listen.

In that moment I said, Lord, that's what I want; I want to know You. I want to hear Your voice. So the next night, I did the same thing. I found out that God—the Creator of the Universe—wanted to talk to me, too. I was lit up! You see, I knew in my head that the Bible says that I would hear my Shepherd's voice, but I did not know it in my heart because I had never experienced it before.

So if you find yourself excited, stirred in your spirit and hungry for more; then you are in the right place.

The Bible says:

> **Matthew 5:6 (NIV)**
> Blessed are those who hunger and thirst for
> righteousness, for they will be filled.

> **Matthew 5:8 (NIV)**
> Blessed are the pure in heart,
> for they will see God.

God created us in His image. He desires a relationship with us. Hearing God's voice brings us into a closer relationship with Him. Just as we desire intimacy with our spouse and with others, God desires an intimacy that is unique to each person individually. He loves us *so much*!

# Chapter One

# The Bible— Our Foundation

What does the Bible say about hearing the voice of God?

**1 Samuel 3:3–10 (NKJV)**
**The Lord Calls Samuel**

³ and before the lamp of God went out in the tabernacle of the Lord where the ark of God was, and while Samuel was lying down, ⁴ that the Lord called Samuel. And he answered, "Here I am!" ⁵ So he ran to Eli and said, "Here I am, for you called me."

And he said, "I did not call; lie down again." And he went and lay down.

⁶ Then the Lord called yet again, "Samuel!"

So Samuel arose and went to Eli, and said, "Here I am, for you called me." He answered, "I did not call, my son; lie down again." ⁷ (Now Samuel did not yet know the Lord, nor was the word of the Lord yet revealed to him.)

⁸ And the Lord called Samuel again the third time. So he arose and went to Eli, and said, "Here I am, for you did call me."

Then Eli perceived that the Lord had called the boy.
⁹ Therefore Eli said to Samuel, "Go, lie down; and it
shall be, if He calls you, that you must say, 'Speak,
Lord, for Your servant hears.'" So Samuel went and
lay down in his place.
¹⁰ Now the Lord came and stood and called as at
other times, "Samuel! Samuel!"

And Samuel answered, "Speak, for Your servant hears."

So Samuel was lying in bed, and he heard the Lord's voice;
it was so clear that he thought it was Eli. At first Eli sort-of
brushed it off, but when it happened the third time, Eli realized that the Lord was calling Samuel. I'm reminded of Matthew 18:3 that says we are to "become like little children."

A friend told me that the first time she heard what she considered to be an audible voice from the Lord, it sounded like
her earthly Father. Obviously, she knew the voice of her own
father. The voice she heard was not out loud like you would
speak to someone audibly, but it was so clear that she thought
it was her father. Samuel heard the Lord's voice, but he thought
it was Eli's voice. Sometimes when the Lord speaks, it could
sound in your ears like the voice of someone you know.

But what does the Bible say about hearing? I was not raised
to hear God's voice in this way. I grew up in church hearing
sermons, memorizing scripture, and reading the Bible with
the understanding of the importance of evangelism. What I
was really being given was a solid foundation that God would
build upon through the years.

One of my earliest memories of hearing and recognizing
the voice of God was through the working of the Holy Spirit
through the gift of discerning of spirits. I know this now to
be a way the Lord speaks, but at the time, I didn't understand. My friends would call me paranoid or fearful. Somehow I knew in my heart that what I was experiencing was not

paranoia but rather that something or someone was telling me not to go there, not to move ahead, or to get out of there quick. Somehow I just knew, even though I did not understand.

I'm so grateful that the Lord, in His infinite wisdom, knew the perfect time to bring mentors into my life. As people moved in and out of my life, God would use them to deposit new truths and then build upon the solid foundation that He had already laid.

Over the years, through intimacy with God, He has taught me to hear His voice in many ways and specifically to hear His voice as if I were sitting and having coffee and talking with a dear friend. I love this kind of relationship. Jesus will always talk to me. He loves to have intimate conversations with me. He loves to just be with me, and I love to be in His presence.

It is my hope for you in reading this book that you develop a relationship with Jesus that you have never had. For those of you that already hear His voice, I pray that a new level of hearing and recognizing the Lord's voice will take place in your life. If this is your first time hearing the Lord's voice, I pray that as a whole new world is opened to you, that you will embrace all that God has for you.

### Mark 10:14–15 (NKJV)

[14] But when Jesus saw it, He was greatly displeased and said to them, "Let the little children come to Me, and do not forbid them; for of such is the kingdom of God. [15] Assuredly, I say to you, whoever does not receive the kingdom of God as a little child will by no means enter it."

I pray for all of us that we will come before Him like a child with child-like faith, and that we never lose our wonder and awe of who the Lord is.

## John 10:1–16 (NKJV)
### Jesus the True Shepherd

[1] "Most assuredly, I say to you, he who does not enter the sheepfold by the door, but climbs up some other way, the same is a thief and a robber. [2] But he who enters by the door is the shepherd of the sheep. [3] To him the doorkeeper opens, and the sheep hear his voice, and he calls his own sheep by name and leads them out. [4] And when he brings out his own sheep, he goes before them, and the sheep follow him, for they know his voice. [5] Yet they will by no means follow a stranger, but will flee from him, for they do not know the voice of strangers." [6] Jesus used this illustration, but they did not understand the things which He spoke to them.

[7] Then Jesus said to them again, "Most assuredly, I say to you, I am the door of the sheep. [8] All who ever came before Me are thieves and robbers, but the sheep did not hear them. [9] I am the door. If anyone enters by Me, he will be saved, and will go in and out and find pasture. [10] The thief does not come except to steal, and to kill, and to destroy. I have come that they may have life, and that they may have it more abundantly.

[11] "I am the good shepherd. The good shepherd gives His life for the sheep. [12] But a hireling, he who is not the shepherd, one who does not own the sheep, sees the wolf coming and leaves the sheep and flees, and the wolf catches the sheep and scatters them. [13] The hireling flees because he is a hireling and does not care about the sheep. [14] I am the good shepherd, and I know My sheep, and am known by My own. [15] As the Father knows Me, even so I know the

Father, and I lay down My life for the sheep. <sup>16</sup> And other sheep I have which are not of this fold; them also I must bring, and they will hear My voice, and there will be one flock and one shepherd."

✧ ✧ ✧ *you can't follow if you can't hear*!

**John 10:27 (NKJV)**
[ <sup>27</sup> My sheep hear My voice, and I know them, and they follow Me. ]

John, chapter 10, talks about the relationship between the Shepherd (Jesus) and the sheep (Believers). The word "know" in John 10:6 is the Greek word *ginosko* that means "to know" and carries connotations of personal covenant knowledge— even marital, one-flesh intimacy. When you read this, you see a simple trust by the sheep to follow the Shepherd. It says, "My sheep hear My voice, and I know them and they follow Me." This really depicts a close, intimate relationship.

When I was attending college, I worked part-time as a bank teller. We were taught to pay attention to possible counterfeit bills coming into the bank. They did not train us to recognize the counterfeit bills; instead, they taught us every detail about the authentic bills. In this way, when a counterfeit bill came across, we would immediately recognize it. In the same way, the more that you get to know the Lord, the easier it will be to spot the counterfeit—the thief, the robber.

Curtis and I will be married thirty-three years this year. Over that period of time, we have become more "in tune" with each other. It did not happen overnight. It took both of us spending time with one another on a *daily* basis to begin to truly hear the heartbeat of the other person. The point is: we had to put time into the relationship in order to get to know one another.

Just like any relationship with a spouse or a friend, you have to spend time together. It is the same with the Lord; you must spend time with Him to hear His voice and to hear His heartbeat.

When you know Jesus, you will also know the Father.

### John 5:19 (NKJV)

Then Jesus answered and said to them, "Most assuredly, I say to you, the Son can do nothing of Himself, but what He sees the Father do; for whatever He does, the Son also does in like manner.

✿ ✿ ✿

### John 14:7 (NKJV)

"If you had known Me, you would have known My Father also, and from now on you know Him and have seen Him."

✿ ✿ ✿

### John 14:20 (NKJV)

At that day you will know that I am in My Father, and you in Me, and I in you.

If we are to hear, then we must listen. That is a key word. When you are with the Lord, don't do all of the talking. How can you hear if you are never quiet? You will find that when you take the time to hear Him, that He has so much to say to you—so much wisdom—so much love.

Wouldn't you like to live in such a close relationship with your Heavenly Father that you could ask Him anything, and He would answer you? Well, Jesus wants to have that kind of relationship with you just as much as you would like to, if not more. How do we know that? Let's look at the first relationships. First, Genesis 1:26 says *"Let Us."* Who is *Us*?

### Genesis 1:1-2 (NKJV)

¹ In the beginning God created the heavens and the earth. ² The earth was without form, and void, and darkness was on the face of the deep. And the Spirit of God was hovering over the face of the waters.

✿ ✿ ✿

### John 1:1–2 (NKJV)

¹ In the beginning was the Word, and the Word was with God, and the Word was God. ² He was in the beginning with God.

According to Genesis 1:1–2, God and the Holy Spirit are present together in the beginning. John 1:1 says *"In the beginning was the Word."* Verse 2 says *"He was in the beginning with God."* We know that Jesus is the Word. So, all three were present in the beginning. God, Jesus, and the Holy Spirit are three different people; yet they are one person. They have a relationship with one another. We were created in their image to look like them, to be in relationship with them, and to also be in relationship with others.

Let's look at what took place in the first relationships in the garden.

### Genesis 1:26–27 (NKJV)

²⁶ Then God said, "Let us make mankind in our image, in our likeness, so that they may rule over the fish in the sea and the birds in the sky, over the livestock and all the wild animals and over all the creatures that move along the ground." So God created mankind in his own image, in the image of God he created them; male and female he created them.

✧   ✧   ✧

**Genesis 3:8 (NKJV)**
Then the man and his wife heard the sound of the
Lord God as he was walking in the garden in the
cool of the day, and they hid from the Lord God
among the trees of the garden.

The next thing we see is that God was walking in the garden
looking for Adam and Eve. The Lord called out to them.  It
wasn't that He didn't know where they were, but His intention
was to speak with them, to have a relationship with them.

Let's look at another patriarch, Moses: Psalm 103:7 (NKJV)
says, "He made known His ways to Moses, His acts to the
children of Israel." What does that mean? Well, the Israelites
knew his acts. They had seen the parting of the Red Sea. They
had seen manna rain down from heaven. They watched as bitter water was turned into sweet, drinkable water. They were
led by a pillar of cloud by day and a pillar of fire by night. You
see, they were acquainted with His supernatural acts, but they
did not know him personally. Moses knew God personally.
The children of Israel had the same opportunity to hear God's
voice, to know Him personally, but they chose not to hear
for themselves. They wanted Moses to speak to them and not
God (Exodus 20:18–19).

Psalm 103:7 (NLT) says, "He revealed his character to Moses
and his deeds to the people of Israel. That says that Moses
knew his character. The more time you spend with someone,
the more their character will be revealed to you. Moses spent
time talking with the Lord. Gideon, David, Solomon, Moses,
and many others had a relationship with God. They were
each given instructions, and they followed them. They had to
"hear" in some way.

So you can see from all of these examples that God's desire is to be in a relationship with us. We were created to be like Him and to be with Him.

Now, let's go back to where we started in John. My sheep—if you're a Christian, a believer, then you're a sheep. He's talking about you.

### John 10:27 (NKJV)
"My sheep hear My voice and I know them and they know Me."

*do you know what you believe?*

☼   ☼   ☼

### John 10:5 (NKJV)
5 Yet they will by no means follow a stranger, but will flee from him, for they do not know the voice of strangers."

This does not mean that they don't hear the voice of strangers (plural); they just know the Shepherd's voice so well that they recognize the voice of strangers and they run from it. There is only one way to have that kind of relationship with the Lord—you have to spend time with Him and get to know Him.

If I want to know how my husband's day went, I have to spend time talking with him. I have to listen to him. I have to give him time to speak to me, filling me in on the details of his day. I can't just acknowledge that he's home and go my way and expect that I will know all about his day. I have to spend time with him.

I think one of the biggest hindrances of any relationship is the struggle to find or make quality time for one another. If that's a struggle for you, ask the Lord how you can make a change in your life to have more quality time with the ones you love. We all struggle with managing our time. Just as we are good stewards of our talents and money; let's also be good stewards of the time we have here on earth.

Time is short! There are many souls to be saved! So let's spend time with God. Let's get His directives and His wisdom for our families, businesses, ministries, relationships, and every aspect of our lives—not just our own.

> Proverbs 8:17 (NKJV)—I love those who love Me, and those who seek Me diligently will find Me.

*God pairs conditions & promises*

☼  ☼  ☼

Matthew 7:7 (NKJV) <u>Ask</u> and it will be <u>given</u> to you, <u>seek</u> and you will <u>find</u>. Knock and it will be <u>opened</u> to you.

☼  ☼  ☼

Matthew 7:8 (NKJV) For everyone who asks receives, and he who seeks finds, and to him who knocks, it will be opened.

*Prov. 4:20-22*

*if you set your mind on things above, what all do you have?*

*when you find out who you are, satan has to prowl somewhere else*

## Chapter Two

# How This Began with Our Son

When my son, Keith, was eight years old, he was having recurring fears every night. With some good ol' detective work (parenting), we discovered where these seeds were planted. Keith had been over at a friend's house and had watched a scary movie, which he was not allowed to watch in our home. Very quickly, the torment began. Each night for weeks, he would come in our room, feeling very fearful, and he would tell us that there was someone standing outside of his bedroom window with a gun.

My husband, Curtis, and I would take turns showing him that there was no one there, while at the same time comforting him by holding him in our arms, holding his hand, and so on. We would unlock the front door, holding his hand the entire time, walk him over to the window, and physically show him that no one was there. We would show him that if someone were by his window, the security lights would turn on. Then we would walk back inside, lock the door, tuck him back into bed, and pray with him. He would fall asleep that night. Then the next evening, we would hear the sound of Keith's footsteps walking into our bedroom to start the whole routine over again.

Finally out of my exasperation, I cried out to the Lord: What do I do? In my mind, it was a rhetorical question because we had been doing what we knew to do, but again, God is always listening to our heart's cry. As clear as a bell, the Lord replied, "Teach him to hear My voice." I said, "Okay. How do I do that?

The following is the conversation between the Lord, Keith, and me.

Cindy: "Lord, what do I do?"

The Lord: "Have Keith sit at the counter and tell him what you are about to do."

Cindy: "Keith, I am going to teach you how to hear the Lord's voice. Would you like to know how to do that?"

Keith: "Yes."

I'm thinking, yeah, I would like to know, too. (I'm really walking by faith in this moment.) At this point in my life, I heard the Lord's voice, but I had no idea how to communicate that to someone else.

Cindy: "Keith, I'm going to have you ask the Lord a question out loud. It is going to be a question that you already know the answer to, but this will make it easier for you to recognize His voice."

Keith: "Okay."

Cindy: "Keith, ask Jesus if He died on the cross for your sins."

Keith: "Jesus, did you die on the cross for my sins?"

Cindy: "What did you hear?"

Keith: "I didn't hear anything."

This is when I realized that I had to teach for a moment. He was only eight years old at the time, and I think he was expecting to hear a person's voice.

Cindy: "Keith, it is not going to be a voice that you hear out loud (which is what he was expecting). It is going to come to you like a thought in your mind. You have thoughts all the time. Right?"

Keith: "Yes."

Cindy: "God is going to speak to your heart, but it will come through your mind as a thought."

Keith: "Okay."

Cindy: "Does that make sense?"

Keith: "Yes."

Cindy: "Okay. We're going to ask the Lord the same question, but this time, you are going to pay attention to the first thought that comes to your mind. Now, close your eyes. Ask Jesus if He died on the cross for your sins."

Keith: "Jesus, did you die on the cross for my sins? (A big smile came over his face as his eyes were closed.)"

Cindy: "What did you hear?"

Keith: "He said that He did."

(Wow! I'm pretty blown away! He had such a sweet smile on his face.)

"Cindy: "Okay. Close your eyes. Jesus, do you love me?"

Keith: "Jesus, do you love me?"

Cindy: "What did He say?"

Keith: (Huge smile) "He said that He did."

I will never forget the smile that came across his face along with the way that he stated his answer. This little eight year old was amazed that Jesus was talking to him. So now I'm thinking—Okay, Lord, what else do I ask?

The Lord: "Ask him if there is anyone outside of his window."

Cindy: "Keith, ask Jesus if there is a man outside of your bedroom window with a gun."

Keith: "Jesus, is there a man outside of my bedroom window with a gun?"

Cindy: "What did you hear?"

Keith: "He said no, there's nobody there."

Cindy: "Ask Jesus where He will be when you're sleeping."
Keith: "Jesus, where will you be when I am sleeping?"
Cindy: "What did He say?"
Keith: "He said He will be right there beside me."

At this point, Keith was peaceful, smiling, and happy. With this newfound joy in his heart, he jumped up from the chair and proceeded to get into bed. I tucked him in, kissed him, and said good night. I didn't have to pray over him or for him because he had just received all that he needed straight from the Lord Himself—Truth. You see, Curtis and I had told him the same thing over and over, but when you hear the truth from the Lord yourself, this changes your life.

That night served many purposes—sleep, peaceful sleep for the household, but most importantly, it was a lesson that Curtis and I were taught that would forever change our lives. We have learned through this to not limit God. He is far more capable of doing so much more than we can possibly conceive.

I think that I've always believed in my head what the Bible teaches about hearing, but because I'd never experienced it, it remained in the head knowledge category of my life. The experience that night moved my heart into a place of being "open" to the things of God. If we will open our hearts, He is sure to fill us with more of Him and surprise us in ways that we cannot imagine.

If you are reading this and are thinking (like I did) that kids can't hear like that—or better yet, people can't hear like that—let me encourage you to search out what the Bible says. Be open to something new in your life. The Bible says in Matthew 18:3 (NCV), "Then he said, "I tell you the truth, you must change and become like little children. Otherwise, you will never enter the kingdom of heaven."

We are not talking about salvation here but rather receiving the Kingdom. Jesus is the Kingdom! He is saying that we must become like a child. What does that mean? To me, one of the greatest traits of children is faith. If you tell them something, they just believe.

Let me give you an example: When the boys were little, they would rough-house with Curtis. They loved to play with their daddy. He would throw them up in the air and then catch them. They would laugh and say, "Do it again. Do it again, Daddy." Not once did it ever cross their minds that their daddy would not catch them. They had "faith" that he would catch them; so they kept coming back for more. It is the kind of faith that our Heavenly Father is looking for in us. The boys did not watch their brother being thrown up into the air and calculate how far Curtis was throwing them, or how long it would take to catch them, or even stop to think—what if he doesn't catch me when it's my turn? That never crossed their minds.

The Lord wants us to come before Him with an expression of child-like faith that says: I don't even understand it all, but I know this—I can't wait for You to hold me in Your arms. I trust You to throw me or propel me into the place that You have for me, and I trust You to be there to catch me at every landing.

**Matthew 7:7–11 (NKJV)**
[7] "Ask, and it will be given to you; seek, and you will find; knock, and it will be opened to you. [8] For everyone who asks receives, and he who seeks finds, and to him who knocks it will be opened. [9] Or what man is there among you who, if his son asks for bread, will give him a stone? [10] Or if he asks for a fish, will he give him a serpent? [11] If you then, being evil, know how to give good gifts to your children, how much more will your Father who is in heaven give good things to those who ask Him!"

So let's begin your journey today with your Heavenly Father. Get your journal out and your pen ready. Let's ask the Lord some of the same questions that Keith asked Him. Write down the question; then close your eyes. Focus on the Lord, and listen with your spiritual ears to hear what the Spirit is saying.

# *Journaling Questions*

1. Jesus, did You die on the cross for me?
2. Jesus, because I have accepted You as my Savior, is heaven now my home?
3. Jesus, do You love me?
4. What do You love about me?

Now, take some time to just be with the Lord. Meditate on the Rhema (spoken) words that he has just spoken to you. Receive His love. Thank Him for opening your spiritual eyes and ears to receive all that He has for you.

① yes
② forever!
③ yes
④ you're mine

# Notes

God's voice isn't necessarily an immediate worded response - scripture is His breath itself. any correct application of His word *is* His voice.

# Chapter Three

# Practical Steps to Begin Hearing the Voice of God

According to Wikipedia, the Gospel of John identifies the *Logos*, through which all things are made, as divine, and further identifies Jesus as the incarnate *Logos*. Vine's Dictionary states that *Logos* means Word. It is the message from the Lord, delivered with His authority and made effective by His power.

So when we are talking about the *Logos* Word of God, we are talking about the written Word or we are talking about Jesus. Here are a few examples of scriptures that refer to the *Logos* Word of God.

**John 1:1–2 (NKJV)**
[1] In the beginning was the Word, and the Word was with God, and the Word was God. [2] He was in the beginning with God.

✧   ✧   ✧

**John 1: 14 (NKJV)**
[1] And the Word became flesh, and dwelt among us, and we saw His glory, glory as of the only begotten from the Father, full of grace and truth.

✧   ✧   ✧

**Hebrews 4:12 (NKJV)**
[12] For the word of God is living and powerful, and sharper than any two-edged sword, piercing even to the division of soul and spirit, and of joints and marrow, and is a discerner of the thoughts and intents of the heart.

Wikipedia states that *Rhema* is a Greek word which literally means an "utterance" or "thing said," and "*Rhema* is the revealed Word of God, as an utterance from God to the heart of the receiver via the Holy Spirit, as in John 14:26."

**John 14:26 (NKJV)**
[26] But the Helper, the Holy Spirit, whom the Father will send in My name, He will teach you all things, and bring to your remembrance all things that I said to you.

When we are talking about *Rhema* words, we are talking about the spoken Word of God. Here are a few examples of scriptures that refer to the *Rhema* Word of God.

**Luke 5:1–8 (NKJV)**
[5] So it was, as the multitude pressed about Him to hear the word of God, that He stood by the Lake of Gennesaret, [2] and saw two boats standing by the lake, but the fishermen had gone from them and were washing their nets. [3] Then He got into one of the boats, which was Simon's, and asked him to put out a little from the land. And He sat down and taught the multitudes from the boat. [4] When He had stopped speaking, He said to Simon, "Launch out into the deep and let down

your nets for a catch." ⁵ But Simon answered and said to Him, "Master, we have toiled all night and caught nothing; nevertheless at Your word I will let down the net." ⁶ And when they had done this, they caught a great number of fish, and their net was breaking. ⁷ So they signaled to their partners in the other boat to come and help them. And they came and filled both the boats, so that they began to sink. ⁸ When Simon Peter saw it, he fell down at Jesus' knees, saying, "Depart from me, for I am a sinful man, O Lord!"

✿   ✿   ✿

**Acts 11:16 (NKJV)**
¹⁶ Then I remembered the word of the Lord, how He said, John indeed baptized with water, but you shall be baptized with the Holy Spirit.

When I first began to hear the Lord's voice, I heard a lot of words of affirmation—I love you, and that sort of thing. It seemed as though for a year or so that the Lord was building me up personally. He would tell me daily that He loved me. Sometimes in one setting, He would tell me two or three times that He loved me. I guess I just needed to hear those words. I've heard that it takes thirteen positive remarks to undo one negative remark. That's probably why we all need to hear over and over—I love you.

We have always made it a point to tell our children over and over that we love them. We feel like our home should be the safe place, the sanctuary filled with love away from the world. I can remember the boys coming in the door after a day at school. I could see the need for affirmation all over them. I would hug them, tell them that I love them, and continue to affirm them as persons. Regardless of the lies that had been spoken over them during the day, my job was to undo those words with affirmation and love. So if we do that for our children, how much more does our Heavenly Father want to affirm His love for us? I don't know about you, but it makes me feel good when I hear Him say that He loves me.

> **Luke 11:11–13 (NKJV)**
> [11] If a son asks for bread from any father among you, will he give him a stone? Or if he asks for a fish, will he give him a serpent instead of a fish? [12] Or if he asks for an egg, will he offer him a scorpion? [13] If you then, being evil, know how to give good gifts to your children, how much more will your Heavenly Father give the Holy Spirit to those who ask Him!"

A lot of people have grown up in environments where all they have ever heard, seen, or experienced were negative words spoken over them or about them. It's no wonder that God would want to tell us over and over that we are loved. He wants us to believe it. When we truly believe that we are loved by our Heavenly Father, then we can walk in the same love that He has given us. When we know that we are loved and we know whose we are—*wow*! Look out! We will set the world on fire with the love of God. After all, God is love. "He who does not love does not know God, for God is love" (1 John 4:8 NKJV).

*Creativity*

We were created in the image of the Lord (Genesis 1:27). All creation came through the Lord. He is where our creativity comes from in the first place. Imagination is in the arena of creativity. Some scientists call it right-brain or left-brain thinking. The way that people tend to process information is usually more on one hemisphere than the other. The right part of the brain is more creative, whereas the left part of the brain tends to be more logical. People who perceive things as only right and wrong, black or white, are usually considered left-brain thinkers. Engineers are great examples of left-brain thinkers. Praise God for their incredible gifts! On the other hand, right-brain thinkers tend to be more creative in nature and have great imaginations. Artists and musicians are great examples of right-brain thinkers. Praise God for their incredible gifts! Some people are a little of both. Personally, I tend to be more right brain, where my husband is both analytical and creative. He's a custom cabinetmaker. He designs and he builds. He handles the smallest to the largest details when customizing a kitchen or any type of cabinetry. His attention to detail is amazing; yet he is still artistic in his design—analytical yet creative.

Why is any of this important to know? Well, I believe it takes a little stress off of us when it comes to hearing the voice of God. Don't be hard on yourself if it seems uncomfortable or difficult at first. What I have discovered in my journey to hear the Lord's voice is that someone who tends to be more creative or imaginative seems to have an easier time hearing the Lord's voice. People who are more logical or analytical tend to use reasoning. That kind of hearing is not tangible, and it simply doesn't seem comfortable or logical. Imagination and creativity are not as logical.

The reason I bring up imagination is because many people see with their spiritual eyes into the Spirit. Some people see pictures of someone or something, scenes—or words. For some it may be like a movie scene. I believe this is easier for them because they are more imaginative than a left-brain thinker. I'm not saying that left-brain thinkers cannot see or hear easily—some can, but many just have to press through a little more. So whether you are left or right brain, I want to show you how to move from logic into the creative flow. We are going to talk about this in more detail in the next few chapters.

Let's get started. At this point, you will want to have a notebook or journal and a pen.

The first thing you have to do is quiet yourself down. Find a place away from the distractions of the world. Shut off the electronics and just sit quietly before the Lord.

Now, if you're like most of us, as soon as you sit down, your mind will start to go to the list of things you need to do for the day, people you need to call, and so forth. You want to get all of those things off your mind so that you can be with the Lord. There are many ways to shift your attention to the Lord—read scripture, worship, put some worship music on. For me, the best way to turn off the left side of my brain is to pray in the Spirit.

### Ephesians 6:17–18 (NKJV)

17 Take the helmet of salvation and the sword of the Spirit, which is the word of God. 18 And pray in the Spirit on all occasions with all kinds of prayers and requests. With this in mind, be alert and always keep on praying for all the Lord's people.

At this point, I have my journal and pen ready to go. As I am praying in the Spirit, I'll begin to hear words or scripture. I'll begin to write what I am hearing in my mind, but I'm listening with my heart, or my spirit. My mind is where the thoughts flow into. Sometimes I will see a picture of something. So I will then ask the Lord what He wants me to know about what I saw. I ask a lot of questions of the Lord. He already knows what I'm thinking, so why not voice it to Him? As far as asking questions of the Lord --anything goes. There is nothing I cannot ask Him. It doesn't mean that I will always hear what I want to, but I still have the freedom to ask Him. That's the kind of relationship He wants to have with us. Jesus was—is—and will always be relational. That is who He is, and that is what He desires for us—relationship and intimacy.

The first relationship that Jesus had was with the Father and the Holy Spirit; theirs has always existed. When Jesus came to earth, He displayed through His life what relationships with others should look like (Gen. 1:1–3; John 1:1; Heb. 13:8).

He chose twelve disciples to walk alongside of Him during his three years of ministry. They ate together, laughed together, and lived life together. He also had other friends just like we do. He shared their sorrows and their joys. Jesus experienced emotions just like we do (John 11:28–33, John 3:16–17, Matt. 9:9–13).

He did not live His life in isolation. He was in relationship with His Father and the Holy Spirit while He was here on this earth. At the same time, He had relationships with other people. Just as Jesus had a relationship with the Lord, we, too, are called to be in relationship with the Lord. Jesus does not want us to "do life" alone.

Another thing that we have to get past in order to hear the Lord's voice is religious thinking. If you were raised in a religious lifestyle, to ask the Lord anything may seem wrong. Religion is a lifestyle that requires you to live under rules and regulations. Jesus was not religious; He was relational. It was the religious leaders who had Him nailed to the cross. Jesus Christ did not come to destroy the law; He came to fulfill it. He was the only one who could.

### Matthew 5:17–20 (NKJV)

[17] "Do not think that I came to destroy the Law or the Prophets. I did not come to destroy but to

fulfill. [18] For assuredly, I say to you, till heaven and earth pass away, one jot or one tittle will by no means pass from the law till all is fulfilled. [19] Whoever therefore breaks one of the least of these commandments, and teaches men so, shall be called least in the kingdom of heaven, but whoever does and teaches them, he shall be called great in the kingdom of heaven. [20] For I say to you, that unless your righteousness exceeds the righteousness of the scribes and Pharisees, you will by no means enter the kingdom of heaven.

When Jesus died on the cross, He fulfilled the law. We no longer had to depend on a prophet to hear directly from God. Salvation through Jesus brought grace – unmerited favor with God. Grace gave us freedom from the law. The cross opened the door for us to hear directly from God. When Jesus died, the temple veil was torn in two from the top to the bottom, symbolizing that we no longer had to go through a prophet or priest; now we can speak directly to the High Priest—Jesus Christ.

### Matthew 27:51 (NKJV)
Then, behold, the veil of the temple was torn in two from top to bottom, and the earth quaked, and the rocks were split.

Praise God! That's great news to me!

So if this rattles your theology, start your journaling right there. Ask the Lord if it is okay to hear His voice. Ask the Lord if reading His Word is the only way to hear Him. Ask the Lord what He wants you to know about you and religion. I promise that He desires to speak to you. He wants to hear from you, and He wants to be in a close relationship with you. Why? Because He loves you. He loves you so much that He sent His only Son to reconcile you to Himself.

You see, Adam gave dominion over to the devil for the knowledge of good and evil. What Adam didn't realize was that he also gave up intimacy with the Lord. It took Jesus Christ to redeem what Adam and Eve had done. When they sinned, it destroyed the close relationship they had with God. They could no longer enjoy their intimate walks and talks in the garden. What they had once shared with the Lord was now cut off because of sin.

### Romans 5:18–19 (NKJV)
[18] Therefore, as through one man's offense judgment came to all men, resulting in condemnation, even so through one Man's righteous act the free gift came to all men, resulting in justification of life. [19] For as by one man's disobedience many were made sinners, so also by one Man's obedience many will be made righteous.

✿   ✿   ✿

### Romans 5:18–19 Amplified Bible (AMP)
[18] Well then, as one man's trespass [one man's false step and falling away led] to condemnation for all men, so one Man's act of righteousness [leads] to acquittal and right standing with God and life for all men.
[19] For just as by one man's disobedience (failing to hear, heedlessness, and carelessness) the many were constituted sinners, so by one Man's obedience the many will be constituted righteous (made acceptable to God, brought into right standing with Him).

Jesus saved us through His death, burial, and resurrection. He provided healing for us by the stripes on His back. When we ask Jesus to come into our hearts, He comes and lives in our heart—our spirit. The spirit is where we hear Him. It is because of Jesus that we can stand righteous before God. We can now walk and talk with Him in the cool of the day. Jesus restored the opportunity for intimacy with the Most High when He died for you and me.

Adam walked in the garden and spoke to God. Even though we don't see God physically, we can see Him with spiritual eyes.

Praise God! Aren't you glad we have the opportunity to be in His presence? Don't let the opportunity of hearing what your Heavenly Father wants to speak to you get away. Now is the time!

Colossians 3:2 (NKJV) tells us to "Set your mind on things above, not on things on the earth." This does not mean to be so spiritually minded that you are of no earthly value, but how about going to the Lord and asking Him to direct our day? Why not ask for His wisdom in our life? Ask Him how we should respond to a situation at work, at home, with our children, and so on.

My prayer for you as you take this journey is that you, too, will get to a place where you are able to talk about everything with the Lord. He already knows every detail of your life. Why not get counsel from the greatest Counselor?

# *Journaling Questions*

1. Lord, is it okay to hear Your voice?
2. Lord, is reading the Bible the only way to hear You?
3. Lord, what are some of the ways that You speak to me?
4. Lord, what do You want me to know about You and religion?

① yes!

② no, i want to speak to you personally

③ writing, head

④ am i receiving what was done on the cross? if not, im living religiously instead of living relationally

# Notes

# Chapter Four

# Two-Way Journaling

Sometimes when I'm talking to a person, I'll ask them if they journal. Many times they will say that they do every day. After we have talked about it for a while, I realize that they journal in diary form—one-way journaling. A diary is a book/journal that you use to write down personal things about yourself, your day, your feelings, your interactions with others, and so forth. Many people use it as a safe place to vent their frustrations. Regardless of what information you put in a diary, it is still a one-way conversation.

For purposes of this book, when I talk about journaling, I am referring to having a two-way conversation with the Lord. It may start with a question, and then the Lord will answer what I have asked. I will write down both my question and His response to me in my journal. The other thing I do when I'm journaling is I will write the month, day, and year in the top right-hand corner of the page. I do this because when I come back to look, I am able to see that on such and such a date, the Lord told me this. I remember asking the Lord one time, "Why do I have to write it down?" He responded, "Because you won't remember." He was right.

One of the benefits of hearing God's voice in my life is to be able to silence the voice of the enemy. For me, this is huge! When the deceiver speaks negative thoughts into my mind, sometimes it will stir my emotions. Sometimes, I'll begin to feel fearful. The only way I know to counter it is by hearing truth from my Father in heaven. Sometimes the enemy will speak a lie, and I will immediately recognize it as a lie. If I've journaled about that particular issue, I can go back in my journal and see that on a certain date, Jesus told me that wasn't true. All of a sudden, faith again rises up within me, and fear begins to move out. Both cannot coexist at the same time. *nyd, what are you trying to bring into coexistance w your faith in God?*

Fear has a way of gripping you so that you don't do the things you know to do—like reading scripture, quoting scripture, worshipping through song, or speaking declarations over yourself. However, when you have God's truth in your life in that situation and in that moment, the lie is vanquished. Fear leaves and peace returns. I don't know about you, but that's enough for me to want to hear my Daddy's voice.

There are different ways of handling spiritual attacks. Sometimes, I'll put on worship music, and after a bit, the oppression or fear leaves.

I grew up being very fearful—not just of one thing, but of everything. It has taken years in my walk with the Lord to break off fear in my life. Sometimes the Lord would allow my circumstances to bring forth faith that I didn't know I had in me. When faith rose up in me, then fear would leave. I remember having anxiety attacks, convinced of a deeper problem. After consulting with a doctor and being told that it was an anxiety attack; I took the doctor's advice and began taking the medicine that he prescribed. That would be a fine solution except for the fact that I needed to function and stay awake—

not sleep. I had three young boys, worked with my husband in our business, served in church, and the list goes on—like most of us.

So I had people tell me to read the Word every time I felt an attack starting, put worship music on, take authority over the enemy, war, and do what you know to do spiritually. And all of these are great suggestions and they do work, but you see, that was the problem: I didn't know what to do spiritually. I knew to read the Word because I knew the Word to be truth and life and sharper than any two-edged sword.

> **Proverbs 4:20–22 (NKJV)**
> [20] My son, give attention to my words;
> Incline your ear to my sayings.
> [21] Do not let them depart from your eyes;
> Keep them in the midst of your heart;
> [22] For they are life to those who find them,
> And health to all their flesh.

✿　✿　✿

> **Hebrews 4:12 (NKJV)**
> For the word of God is living and powerful, and sharper than any two-edged sword, piercing even to the division of soul and spirit, and of joints and marrow, and is a discerner of the thoughts and intents of the heart.

Many times fear would subside, and I would feel peace come over me, but sometimes fear would grip me so much that I could not focus on the Word even though I would read it or quote it out loud. Other times, like Saul, I would put on worship music to soothe my soul. It would leave for a time, but soon it would be back. Once I was filled with the Spirit and received my own prayer language, then I began praying in the Spirit a lot. I found that when I had no clue how to battle or what to say, that the Holy Spirit knew what to pray perfectly. This was my new weapon of warfare to add to the arsenal. The Bible speaks in Ephesians [6] about our weapons. All of them are defensive except for the Word of God and praying in the Spirit. These are the offensive weapons of warfare. We need both!

> **Ephesians 6:17 (NKJV)**
> [17] And take the helmet of salvation, and the sword of the Spirit, which is the word of God; [18] praying always with all prayer and supplication in the Spirit, being watchful to this end with all perseverance and supplication for all the saints.

All of these things together helped me, in the name of Jesus, My Savior, to battle the spirit of fear. I don't think there is only one way to handle a specific situation. I believe God gives us many tools to use at our disposal. We must learn to pull from the wisdom of God and discern what to use at what time and how to use it.

God then began to show me another way to defeat the enemy. Guess what it was? Identifying the lies of the enemy and then allowing the Lord to speak truth to me. This was my new training ground. I love this scripture:

> **John 8:31 (NKJV)**
> [31] Then Jesus said to those Jews who believed Him, "If you abide in My word, you are My disciples indeed. [32] And you shall know the truth, and the truth shall make you free."

✧  ✧  ✧

**John 8:36 (NKJV)**
[36] Therefore if the Son makes you free, you shall be
free indeed.

Indeed means without a doubt; it means certainty. When the
Lord speaks truth into your life, the enemy is defeated. The
lie has no hold on you. Peace moves in, and the enemy cannot hold you in bondage to that lie. That is true freedom in
Christ. Reading the Word is truth. So when you know in your
head the truth of the Word of God and then you hear a Word
from the Lord, it's like a double truth. It's concrete, and no one
is moving you from that truth. Remember the example from
chapter 2 where Curtis and I kept telling our son that there was
no one outside of his window. When Jesus spoke truth to him,
he was immediately set free, and Satan and his tormentors no
longer had a hold on him. He was certainly free indeed.

So when the enemy comes to you and begins to whisper
lies to you like: you're worthless, you're a failure, you'll never
do anything, you can't do that, you'll always be alone, you're
stupid, and so forth (we have all heard them), that's when
you want to get your journal out and sit down and talk to the
Lord. Ask the Lord what lies you are hearing and then ask the
Lord what He says is the truth. Ask the Lord for a scripture
that speaks truth to the lie that you're hearing. By the time you
are finished, you will be encouraged by your Heavenly Father
and ready to take on the world because "greater is He that is
in you than he who is in the world."

**1 John 4:4 (NKJV)**
[4] You are of God, little children, and have overcome
them, because He who is in you is greater than he
who is in the world.

☼   ☼   ☼

**1 John 4:4 (NCV)**

[4] My dear children, you belong to God and have defeated them; because God's Spirit, who is in you, is greater than the devil, who is in the world.

Are there areas in your life that you need to be set free in? It begins with a personal relationship with Christ. Once you are saved, you then pursue intimacy with Jesus Christ. Get to know Him. Read the Bible and you will discover who He is. As you spend time with Him, you will find that He longs to speak to you, and He loves to be with you. He loves you!

# *Journaling Questions*

1. Lord, in what area of my life does the enemy have a hold?
2. What are the lies (plural) that I'm hearing or believing regarding this particular area of my life?
3. Would You speak truth to each lie that I have believed.
4. What else do You want me to know today?

# Notes

# Chapter Five

# The Holy Spirit—
# The Umpire

What role does the Holy Spirit play in hearing the voice of God?

**Isaiah 53:5 (NKJV)**
⁵ But He was wounded for our transgressions,
He was bruised for our iniquities;
The chastisement for our peace was upon Him,
And by His stripes we are healed.

I think there's more to that scripture than we really understand. Why were the soldiers so brutal while beating Jesus? Satan was working through them, and He knew the power of peace—the power of the Holy Spirit. Why did Jesus take this chastisement, according to the Word, for our peace? This particular phrase is worded a little differently in various versions, but when I read the NKJV, it struck me. You know how words in the Bible seem to jump off of the page? Well, God was showing me something about peace. Jesus understood how important peace would be for us in a world of turmoil. His peace, which he had already received at His water baptism, was the same peace that He would leave with us. He paid it *all* for us! Webster's Dictionary says that the word *chastisement* means "painful affliction." That's what Jesus endured so that we could have peace, and so that we could live here on earth with the Holy Spirit, who is peace.

Another way that the Holy Spirit speaks to us is that He will give us perfect peace.

**Isaiah 26:3 (NIV)**
³ You will keep in perfect peace
those whose minds are steadfast,
because they trust in you.

To never read the Bible, the (*Logos*) written Word of God, and only live by (*Rhema*) spoken words from the Lord is out of balance. Our pastor has this saying: every road has two ditches, and each of them is bad. Everything we hear from the Lord must always line up with the Word of God, either by scripture or by principle.

For instance, the Bible doesn't tell me what school my children should attend. Nowhere in the Bible does it say: Curtis and Cindy, put your children in public school, private school, or even home school. What the Bible does say is to bring them up in the discipline and instruction of the Lord. (Eph. 6:4) It is up to us as parents to seek the Lord for what is best for our children and for our family. As we seek the Lord, when we make the decision that God wanted us to make, what happens? We begin to sense a peace come over us in our hearts. That peace is the Holy Spirit. When we make a decision and there is doubt and there is no peace, we must learn to wait until we have the Lord's peace.

As we have grown in Christ through the years, we have learned to wait on the Lord when making decisions. When I was younger, I really thought this principle held true to only big decisions, but I have since learned that we should rely upon the Lord in everything we do. It is prideful on our part to think that we can do things outside of Him because in the end, the things we do will all be weighed by the Lord. And those things that are eternal shall stand, but those that are not will be burned up in the fire (1 Cor. 3:13).

Let me give you another example: Peace is the umpire—the judge. In a baseball game, an umpire is the person that makes the call. If there is any dispute or indecision of any kind, everyone defers to the umpire. In the same way, The Holy Spirit is our Umpire. The Holy Spirit is peace. He will be the peace that umpires in our spirit if we will recognize when He is speaking. Satan can counterfeit pretty much everything, but he cannot counterfeit the peace or love of God. Even when he tries, there's something that is just not quite right. It's because the peace of God is the Holy Spirit.

John 14:16 says that the Holy Spirit is a Helper. Some versions call Him an Advocate. John 16:13 tells us that the Holy Spirit is our Guide. He leads us, and He desires for us to follow His direction. John 14:26 says that the Holy Spirit is a Teacher.

I recently visited the church where my daughter attends college. I noticed in the worship settings that they were not sure where God was going to take them in their worship, but as they pursued Him in worship, the Holy Spirit would lead them and they would follow. It was not just the worship team that flowed in the Spirit like this—they also had artists who would paint at the same time that the worship was going on. It was really quite a prophetic visual of being led by the Spirit of God.

At the beginning of the service, a blank canvas would be set up on the stage. Sometimes there would be up to three different artists preparing to paint for the same service. It was amazing to see the finished product. When the artists would start out, they would have nothing on the canvas, but as the music began, the Holy Spirit began to move in them. They began to paint. I don't understand their specific process, whether they saw the whole picture and began to paint or whether they began in faith with a few paint strokes. Either way, it began with just a few strokes, and then it began to look like something. By the end of the service, we could stand back and see the finished product, which in my opinion, was sometimes breathtaking and absolutely beautiful!

I began to see a theme which, I believe, God was speaking to me. "Step out and pursue the things that God has called you to do. Even if you don't know how you're getting there, just listen for His voice and He will lead you."

Just as the musicians and the artists had natural skills, you, also have skills and abilities that God has given you. God is not calling you to know all of the details of the journey and destination; He is asking you to rely on Him to lead and guide you in the process. He will give you all of the information that you need for the moment. I think if He showed us every detail of our lives at one time, we would be overwhelmed. God is gracious and loving. He gives us what we need to help move us in the direction of our destiny. He does not expect us to know it all; He simply wants us to come to Him and ask. "Ask, and it will be given to you; seek, and you will find; knock, and it will be opened to you" (Matt. 7:7 NKJV).

And give us this day our daily bread—manna. He wants to give us daily what we need, just like He did for the children of Israel in the wilderness. There's no formula. Just be with Him. You'll find that the more you are with Him, the more peaceful you will become.

I can remember hearing that couples that stay together for years begin to look like each other or act like each other. I don't know how literal that is, but it's interesting. Regardless, it's because they've spent a lifetime with their spouse. It's the same with the Lord—the more time we spend with Him, the more we begin to look like Him. It's not just the destination that's important; it's the journey that brings us to the destination that is equally important.

Spend time with the Lord. Listen for His voice. Ask for His wisdom in your life. Worship Him in Spirit and in Truth. You will not be disappointed!

Jesus promised us that He would never leave us alone. In John 16, Jesus tells the disciples that when He is gone, He will send the Holy Spirit to take His place here on the earth. He describes the Holy Spirit as a Helper—some versions say Advocate. If you read on through verse 15, Jesus is letting His disciples know that the Holy Spirit will now speak to us. Jesus is the Mediator between God and men, but the Holy Spirit will make His words known to us.

### 1 Timothy 2:5 (NKJV)
5 For there is one God and one Mediator between God and men, the Man Christ Jesus, He will communicate with us and for us.

According to the Google Dictionary, a mediator is a go-between.

### John 16:12–15 (NKJV)
12 "I have much more to say to you, more than you can now bear. 13 But when he, the Spirit of truth, comes, he will guide you into all the truth. He will not speak on his own; he will speak only what he hears, and he will tell you what is yet to come. 14 He will glorify me because it is from me that he will receive what he will make known to you. 15 All that belongs to the Father is mine. That is why I said the Spirit will receive from me what he will make known to you."

When we speak to the Lord, we are speaking to all three of the Trinity, but we hear through the voice of the Holy Spirit. They are one, yet they are three. They have unity in position but diversity in function. They are all God.

> ### Matthew 3:13–17 (NKJV)
> [13] Then Jesus came from Galilee to John at the Jordan to be baptized by him. [14] And John tried to prevent Him, saying, "I need to be baptized by You, and are You coming to me?" [15] But Jesus answered and said to him, "Permit it to be so now, for thus it is fitting for us to fulfill all righteousness." Then he allowed Him. [16] When He had been baptized, Jesus came up immediately from the water, and behold, the heavens were opened to Him, and He saw the Spirit of God descending like a dove and alighting upon Him. [17] And suddenly a voice came from heaven, saying, "This is My beloved Son, in whom I am well pleased."

In these verses, you see that all three persons of the Trinity are present. Jesus is being baptized. The Holy Spirit descended like a dove and rested upon Him, and the Father spoke from heaven. So here we see that they are one; yet they are three. When we "hear" from the Lord, we are hearing them as one, yet the Holy Spirit is here with us speaking the words of Jesus and the Father. The Holy Spirit is the Comforter that Jesus spoke of in John 16.

This is how we taught our children about the Trinity: God the Father, Jesus the Son, and the Holy Spirit are one person, yet they are three separate people with three different functions.

If I turn on the kitchen faucet, water will begin to pour out. If I put a cup under the faucet, I will have a glass of water. The water represents God the Father. Now if I take that same glass of water and pour half of it into a pan and place it on top of the stove, it is still the same water. As the water begins to boil, it produces steam, which represents the Holy Spirit. It's now steam or vapor, but it's still water. Now if I take some of the water left in the glass and I pour it over an empty ice cube tray, I can freeze that same water. It becomes ice cubes—this represents Jesus. Now, all three of these forms still come from water; yet all three have a different function—that is, water, ice, and steam.

**1 John 5:7–8 (NKJV)**
7 For there are three that bear witness in heaven: the Father, the Word, and the Holy Spirit, and these three are one. 8 And there are three that bear witness on earth: the Spirit, the water, and the blood, and these three agree as one.

So when I'm journaling, Jesus will speak to me through the Holy Spirit. I will hear the Holy Spirit in my spirit, which will be filtered through my mind. My mind is where all of the thoughts are filtered through. It only makes sense that we would hear in the same way. Most of us have been hearing for years but simply did not recognize His voice.

Come Holy Spirit. Teach us to hear and recognize Your voice.

**John 14:26-27 (NKJV)**
26 But the Helper, the Holy Spirit, whom the Father will send in My name, He will teach you all things, and bring to your remembrance all things that I said to you. 27 Peace I leave with you, My peace I give to you; not as the world gives do I give to you. Let not your heart be troubled, neither let it be afraid.

# *Journaling Questions*

1. Holy Spirit, what do You want me to know about You?
2. Holy Spirit, where have I grieved (made You sad) You in my life?
3. Holy Spirit, where have I quenched (said no to You) You in my life?
4. Lord, what else do You want me to know today?

① that i am trustworthy
② disobedience
③ relationships
④ i am there

# Notes

# Chapter Six

# Different Ways to Hear and Recognize the Voice of God

This book is not intended to show you only one way to hear God's voice. We must be open to hearing and recognizing God's voice in many ways and on many levels. God is always communicating, but we are not always listening. We must learn to "tune in" to His voice.

When you get saved, it's like you receive a cell phone. Everything you need for communication and life is available through your phone. A cell phone can't be used to its potential without knowledge of its technical capabilities. The communication is available, but you must access it. The Bible is the manual. There is nothing in this life that you cannot find counsel for in the Bible. The Bible, like your cell phone, has many applications. Your cell phone provides many unlimited resources, as does your Heavenly Father. There is unlimited power that comes through accessing your phone. We must learn how to access and use the information and power. When you first get saved, you have instant technical support, if you desire, in your pastors, leaders, and other believers. They can teach you how to turn on the cell phone. As you attend church, you learn more about the capabilities. As you study the Word, you begin to add more applications which gives you more knowledge and access to the Provider.

Everyone gives you new and different tips on how to use the phone. Before you know it, you are connected and are now teaching others how to use the phone. You're connected with the Provider all the time. The Provider gives you information, which helps you solve problems of your day. God wants to communicate with us. He wants a relationship with us, but we are not always in tune with His voice.

### The Bible

One of my favorite ways to hear the Lord's voice is through reading the *Logos* (written) Word of God. No matter what situation or challenge I am going through in life, I can always open my Bible, and God will speak to me through His Word. I love the Word of God. It is truly life for those who believe. The Bible is the Word of God in written (*Logos*) form. It is sharper than a two-edged sword.

> **Hebrews 4:12 (NKJV)**
> For the word of God is living and powerful, and sharper than any two-edged sword, piercing even to the division of soul and spirit, and of joints and marrow, and is a discerner of the thoughts and intents of the heart.

Have you ever read the Bible and all of a sudden, a scripture seems to jump off of the page? You see or realize something new about that scripture that you didn't know before even though you've read it a hundred times. You understand a depth of that Word, which spoke life to you. It spoke personally to your circumstances in a way that you cannot explain. Well, that's what I call revelation, or understanding, which only comes from the Lord. Revelation is supernatural knowledge given to you from the Lord. You did not get it on your own.

According to the Merriam-Webster Dictionary, revelation is:

1.  An act of revealing or communicating divine truth.
2.  Something that is revealed by God to humans.

No matter how you hear or recognize God's voice, He is the One who gives you revelation in situations and circumstances and revelation of His Word. There are people who "know" what the Bible says in what I call "head knowledge," but they do not really know the depth of what a scripture means. They have not received revelation from the Most High. The Pharisees knew the Law and the words of the prophets, yet they did not have an intimate relationship with the Lord; therefore, they had no revelation of the Word. They did not recognize the Word when He was in front of them. They had knowledge, but the revelation of who Jesus was and His words had not moved to their heart.

We read the Bible for different reasons. One is to allow the Word of God to penetrate our heart, soul, and mind—every part of our being. One day we might be reading the Word and we walk away joyful and encouraged, but on another day, life may put a demand on us to know what we believe. It is in those moments that the Word of God becomes life to us.

## Character of God

We need to know the Word of God so that we know the One who wrote this book. The Bible reveals the character of God. How do you really get to know Him unless you spend time with Him and read His Word? It's not about obtaining knowledge to have knowledge; it's about knowing Him. Through intimacy with Him and knowing Him, we begin to reflect His character in our lives. We begin to look like Him.

Reading His Word also equips us for the moment when life asks the question: What do you really believe? If you have never read the Word, you won't really know what you believe. The world around you will try to tell you what you should believe. How will you filter the world's view of your Heavenly Father if you have nothing to pull from? There are many religions with many philosophies, but there is only one Jesus. When you know who He is, you will know the Father and the Holy Spirit.

When a bride and groom get married, they immediately set aside time for a honeymoon. A honeymoon is a time for them to get to know each other intimately in a way they have not known before. When the honeymoon is over and they return to their home, jobs, and so on, they must continue to make time for one another. In one week or even two, they did not learn all there is to know about the other person. Actually, they will spend their lifetime learning about the character of the one they love.

And so it is with your Heavenly Father. Once you have accepted Christ, there is a honeymoon phase. You are so in awe of what He has done for you and how He has saved you. You still have only scratched the surface of who He is. The intimacy that you develop with the Lord will, in time, reveal His character and who He is. It doesn't happen in a week or two; it will take your lifetime. God is always revealing new things about Himself to us. We just need to listen for His voice.

## Recalling His Word in Our Heart

We also want to read God's Word so that it's in our memory bank, and when we need to draw from it, the Holy Spirit can recall it to our mind. Feed on the Word of God. Store His words in your heart. A day will come when you need to draw from His Word which has been deposited into your heart.

**John 14:26 (NKJV)**
But the Helper, the Holy Spirit, whom the Father will send in My name, He will teach you all things, and bring to your remembrance all things that I said to you.

## Revelation

Another reason, which is huge, that we want to read God's Word is so that God will give revelation (wisdom and understanding) into the scriptures. It always amazes me that I can read the same scripture that I have read many times, but in a specific moment, He reveals something to me that I've never seen or understood before. It's as if I've read that scripture for the first time. A new level of revelation was just revealed. Wow! God is so awesome. He's always teaching, equipping, loving, and speaking in a way that each of us can understand.

Revelation leads us into an experience with God. When we experience God's love, His revelation, His truth, and His hand in our lives, no one can ever take that away from us. It's like salvation; the day you were saved, you had an experience with God's love through Jesus that no one shared except you and the Lord. If someone said to you, you're not really saved; it wouldn't affect you at all. Why? Because you experienced Jesus' love in such a real way that nothing can ever take that experience and truth away from you. That's the power of revelation at work in your life.

## Spiritual Warfare

Another reason to know the Word of God is to defeat the attacks of the enemy.

**Ephesians 6:10–18 (NKJV)**
**The Whole Armor of God**

[10] Finally, my brethren, be strong in the Lord and in the power of His might. [11] Put on the whole armor of God, that you may be able to stand against the wiles of the devil. [12] For we do not wrestle against flesh and blood, but against principalities, against powers, against the rulers of the darkness of this age, against spiritual hosts of wickedness in the heavenly places. [13] Therefore take up the whole armor of God, that you may be able to withstand in the evil day, and having done all, to stand. [14] Stand therefore, having girded your waist with truth, having put on the breastplate of righteousness, [15] and having shod your feet with the preparation of the gospel of peace; [16] above all, taking the shield of faith with which you will be able to quench all the fiery darts of the wicked one. [17] And take the helmet of salvation, and the sword of the Spirit, which is the word of God; [18] praying always with all prayer and supplication in the Spirit, being watchful to this end with all perseverance and supplication for all the saints.

If you look at verses 14–18, you will notice that all of the weapons mentioned here are defensive except for two. The two offensive weapons are the Sword of the Spirit (the Word of God) and praying in the Spirit. God has given us all that we need to defeat the enemy—defensively and offensively.

## Entertaining Angels

Another way we may hear from the Lord is through angels. When angels appear to men, they usually have a message that God wants to communicate to us. Let's first look at an example from the scripture.

### Luke 1:26–38 (NKJV)

²⁶ Now in the sixth month the angel Gabriel was sent by God to a city of Galilee named Nazareth, ²⁷ to a virgin betrothed to a man whose name was Joseph, of the house of David. The virgin's name was Mary. ²⁸ And having come in, the angel said to her, "Rejoice, highly favored one, the Lord is with you; blessed are you among women!"

²⁹ But when she saw him, she was troubled at his saying, and considered what manner of greeting this was. ³⁰ Then the angel said to her, "Do not be afraid, Mary, for you have found favor with God. ³¹ And behold, you will conceive in your womb and bring forth a Son, and shall call His name Jesus. ³² He will be great, and will be called the Son of the Highest, and the Lord God will give Him the throne of His father David. ³³ And He will reign over the house of Jacob forever, and of His kingdom there will be no end."

³⁴ Then Mary said to the angel, "How can this be, since I do not know a man?"

³⁵ And the angel answered and said to her, "the Holy Spirit will come upon you, and the power of the Highest will overshadow you; therefore, also, that Holy One who is to be born will be called the Son of God. ³⁶ Now indeed, Elizabeth your relative has also conceived a son in her old age, and this is now the sixth month for her who was called barren. ³⁷ For with God nothing will be impossible."

³⁸ Then Mary said, "Behold the maidservant of the Lord! Let it be to me according to your word." And the angel departed from her.

✧   ✧   ✧

### Matthew 1:18–24 (NKJV)

[18] Now the birth of Jesus Christ was as follows: After His mother Mary was betrothed to Joseph, before they came together, she was found with child of the Holy Spirit. [19] Then Joseph her husband, being a just man, and not wanting to make her a public example, was minded to put her away secretly. [20] But while he thought about these things, behold, an angel of the Lord appeared to him in a dream, saying, "Joseph, son of David, do not be afraid to take to you Mary your wife, for that which is conceived in her is of the Holy Spirit. [21] And she will bring forth a Son, and you shall call His name Jesus, for He will save His people from their sins."

[22] So all this was done that it might be fulfilled which was spoken by the Lord through the prophet, saying: [23] "Behold, the virgin shall be with child, and bear a Son, and they shall call His name Immanuel," which is translated, "God with us."

What was the message for both Mary and Joseph? "Do not be afraid," the angel said.

God will sometimes use angels to relay a message from Him. We may not recognize them as angels, but sometimes we will—even if it is not until years later. This is my friends' story about their angelic encounter:

Back in 1995, Adair and Kathryn purchased their first home. On the day that they moved in, several friends and family members came to help them unload their moving truck. As the last couple of people were leaving their home that afternoon, Adair walked them to the door to say goodbye.

He watched as they walked down their entry way and to their cars. He closed the door and began walking down the hall to one of their bedrooms. Adair and Kathryn were the only ones in the house at the time. Within a few minutes, the doorbell rang. Adair assumed it was probably one of the people who had just left the house (maybe they had forgotten something).

He went to the door and opened it. Standing there was a boy who was probably twelve or thirteen years old. He was pale skinned with freckles and red hair. He was wearing a red baseball cap. Adair was a little startled, because he was not expecting a visitor within minutes of moving into their new home. He said hello. The boy asked if they had a Band-Aid. The boy pointed to his knee, which was bleeding. He said that he was out bird watching and that he had climbed through a barbed-wire fence to get over to their neighborhood. Adair asked him where he lived, and the boy gestured and said something like "over there." Adair and Kathryn lived in a brand-new neighborhood, which had been a cow pasture; so it did make sense to them that he had climbed through a barbed-wire fence to get into their neighborhood.

Adair went back inside the house and the boy stayed on the front porch. They went inside to look for a Band-Aid. He walked back outside with the Band-Aid. He got down on one knee to put the Band-Aid on the boy. He looked back up at the boy. His head was just in front of the sun, with some light coming around the right side of his face. The light was so bright that he could not see his face anymore. Adair squinted his eyes so that he could see him as they continued to talk. At that point, Adair noticed that he had binoculars around his neck and he was wearing a red shirt. Kathryn stood there as they talked for a few minutes. The young boy asked if they had moved in, and Kathryn said, "Yes, they had just moved in that day." The boy said that they seemed like nice people and that he really appreciated their help.

Kathryn stepped back inside the house as Adair continued to have small talk with him. Her radar was on high alert as the whole situation took place. It seemed very strange to her. After a few minutes, they were standing at the door, and the boy turned to leave. As he walked down the entryway, he turned and said, "Say hello to the kids for me." Kathryn thought that was odd because their children were not at home that day; they were staying with her mom while they moved in. He had not been inside to see any pictures or toys, and they had not discussed their children in any way. So for him to say that seemed odd.

Adair stood inside the house and saw Kathryn standing in the kitchen. She heard what the boy said and had a look on her face that communicated "that was strange." She whispered to Adair, "Which way did he go?" He told her that he had gone left, in front of the garage. The garage door was open and she could see straight out from the kitchen. She told Adair that she could not see him; so she walked from the kitchen out into the garage. From the garage, she walked out to the driveway. Adair walked out the front door at the same time, and they both got to the driveway within a couple of seconds. No one was there (I mean no one). The boy had disappeared. It had only been about five seconds since he had walked away, and now he was not anywhere to be found. They quickly looked on both sides of the house and looked all around. They said that it would be hard to hide in that neighborhood at the time because there were no homes next to them on any side. There were also no trees. It was a newly developed neighborhood with lots of clear space and dirt. The boy was simply not there.

Adair and Kathryn were youth pastors at that time. They had worked with teenagers for several years. It was interesting to them that a teenage boy would show up at their home within minutes of them moving into a new neighborhood and needed their help. Even stranger to them was the boy saying that he was bird watching. How many teenage boys do you know that bird watch and admit it? Then after he talked to them for a few minutes and then told them to "say hello to the kids for me," that was even stranger.

They had always felt that this young boy was an angel; however, it wasn't until thirteen years later that it was definitely confirmed. They were talking to their kids recently about the incident. As Kathryn retold the story, she stated that the boy was a young black teenager; meanwhile, Adair retorted, hmm... "I saw a young white teenager with red hair and freckles."

They believe that God sent an angel to welcome them to their new home and to let them know that He was always watching over them.

This scripture came to mind:

**Hebrews 13:2 (NKJV)**
[2] Do not forget to entertain strangers, for by so doing some have unwittingly entertained angels.

### Strangers

God also speaks through strangers or even unsaved people. God can use anything He wants to in order to turn our hearts over to Him. So don't limit God! His ways are higher than our ways.

When Curtis and I were dating, he was not a Christian. We attended church regularly together. Weekly, he heard the messages from the pastors. He heard the Bible stories and day-to-day illustrations week after week. In other words, he had been exposed to the Word of God. He had been raised in the church when he was younger, but he had not given his heart to the Lord yet.

Curtis was out at a bar with a friend, who at the time was also not a Christian, and some others. They were all sitting at a table. His friend, along with a girl, was sitting across from him. They sat talking while having a few drinks. Curt's friend got up and left the table for a few minutes. As soon as he left, the girl's ex-boyfriend walked up to her at the table and dumped a drink on the top of her head. Curtis immediately stood up to defend the girl, and as soon as he stood up, the guy turned to him and punched him right in the mouth. At that point, Curtis and this guy were going to take their aggressions outside. Curt's friend came back to the table, and said to Curtis, "I bet you think that God did that?" Curt said, "No, I don't think that at all." Again his friend looked right at him and said, "It's almost like that was from God." Curt said, "No, it wasn't." Then his friend said, "It's almost like God punched you right in the mouth." Curtis tried to ignore his friend's words as he walked outside with the other guy.

While Curtis was outside, God spoke to him clearly. The Lord said, "Are you willing to give up everything that everyone here is searching for? I will show you in the Spirit that they are all searching for what you already have. Are you willing to give that up? I'll show you their loneliness, their emptiness." There's more to the story, but eventually, the guy apologized to Curtis and he left.

Curtis went back inside and sat down at the table. From that moment on, he was changed. He sat there looking around and observing everyone in the bar. God was allowing him to see the emptiness within people. He saw how lost many of them were. He could see that they were searching for something. God began speaking to him in the bar that night. He heard His voice and gave his heart to the Lord. He has never looked back. Satan tried to drive him further away from the Lord. God did not cause the incident, but God used a nonbeliever to speak words that would pierce Curt's heart and change his life for eternity.

If you will listen, you will hear God speaking to you. It's His desire for you to hear His voice because He loves you. He loves you so much!

# *Journaling Questions*

1.  Lord, why do You want me to read Your Word?
2.  What will reading Your Word do for me?
3.  Lord, give me an example of a time when You gave me a revelation from Your Word.
4.  What other ways do you speak to me that I'm unaware of?
5.  What else do you want me to know today?

# Notes

# Chapter Seven

# Can We Hear for Others? Can We Prophesy?

**1 Corinthians 14:31 (NKJV)**
For you can all prophesy one by one, that all may learn and all may be encouraged.

What if I missed it? What if what I heard was wrong? Are these my thoughts? Is this from the Lord or is this from Satan? Have you ever asked any of these questions? I'll start by saying that we see and know in part. We live in a fallen world. There is a chasm between heaven and earth. When we get to heaven, everything we hear and see will be pure.

**James 3:17—(NKJV)**
[17] But the wisdom that is from above is first pure, then peaceable, gentle, willing to yield, full of mercy and good fruits, without partiality and without hypocrisy.

James says that the wisdom from above is first pure. According to the Merriam-Webster Dictionary, pure is:

(1)   Not mixed with anything else;
(2)   Clean and not harmful in any way; or

(3)   Having a smooth and clear sound that is not mixed with any other sounds.

The wisdom that comes from above is not mixed with any other sounds. It is pure. It is God's voice—not mine and not the enemy's.

All of this is part of our walk as a Christian. When we were babies, we did not think or act like adults. We had to learn how to crawl, walk and then run. "For now we see in a mirror, dimly, but then face to face. Now I know in part, but then I shall know just as I also am known" (1 Corinthians 13:12 NKJV).

The scripture tells us in James what God's wisdom looks like—pure, peaceable, gentle, willing to yield, full of mercy and good fruits, without partiality and without hypocrisy...

**James 3:13–18 (NKJV)**
**Heavenly Versus Demonic Wisdom**
[13] Who is wise and understanding among you? Let him show by good conduct that his works are done in the meekness of wisdom. [14] But if you have bitter envy and self-seeking in your hearts, do not boast and lie against the truth. [15] This wisdom does not descend from above, but is earthly, sensual, demonic. [16] For where envy and self-seeking exist, confusion and every evil thing are there. [17] But the wisdom that is from above is first pure, then peaceable, gentle, willing to yield, full of mercy and good fruits, without partiality and without hypocrisy. [18] Now the fruit of righteousness is sown in peace by those who make peace.

You are not alone; everyone asks these questions. We all want to make certain that we are hearing God's voice and not being deceived. Continue to go back to the Lord. Continue to journal. Do not allow the fear of failure to cause you to never try again. This is where a prayer partner is so helpful. They can speak into your life and encourage you when you are discouraged.

One thing that we've done with our young adult children is that we will all pray together about a specific prayer request or maybe for a specific person. We listen to hear what the Lord is saying, and then we write it down. Then we read out loud what we heard. Normally, you will see repetitive words, exact sentences or phrases, used in each person's word. This encourages each person and builds their faith that God is speaking and that we are listening and hearing correctly. It also provides accountability within the family setting.

One of my favorite things to do is to ask the Lord for a birthday word for a family member. Our whole family loves to get a birthday word from the Lord. Who wouldn't? Again, each of us will spend time on our own with the Lord and ask Him for an encouraging word for the birthday guy or gal. We then type them up and place them in a new journal for the person. I am always amazed when we type up the words, and we see a common thread or an exact sentence used in each of the different words that were given. No matter how long you have heard your Heavenly Father's voice, it will really excite you and build your faith.

In our family, when our birthdays roll around, we come expecting to see a journal in the midst of presents. I've watched a few times as the kids will look on the coffee table at the wrapped presents. I know exactly what they are looking for— the wrapped present in the shape of a book. When they were younger, they would look for the gifts; however, as they have grown up and matured, they understand the value of a word from the Lord. For us, there is nothing better than a word from the Lord to encourage us on our birthdays. Personally,

I love to go back and look at the previous year's journal and re-read the words. I'm encouraged as I look and see what God has done in my life over one year.

Another aspect of hearing from the Lord is to sense His peace about the word. Let me explain: Sometimes I will sit down to ask the Lord for a word for someone. I'll get halfway through and start to feel as though these are my personal thoughts, and I don't have peace. At that point, I discard the word, and I will wait until another time to hear from the Lord. Sometimes you know the person too well, which makes it harder. Sometimes you're inundated with the "stuff called life" from the world, and you're not focused on the Lord. If I don't have peace; I throw it out and wait. I like to worship, and then when I'm in the presence of God, I'll ask for that word.

On the flipside of getting an encouraging word for someone, what about receiving a word from someone? It is your responsibility to discern whether or not the word is from the Lord. Just because someone says that it's from the Lord; that does not mean that it's true. Most of the time, a prophetic word will confirm what God is already speaking to you in your private time with Him.

Have you ever had this happen? Someone gets a word from God, but then they add onto it. For whatever reason, they feel they have to interpret what He said. Sometimes it's very definitive which part of the word is from the Spirit and which part of the word is from the flesh. Sometimes, though, it seems blurred or mixed together. Personally, I throw the whole thing out unless the Lord tells me otherwise. I trust that if God wants me to know something, then He will tell me. Again, I go back to peace—peace is my umpire. If I don't sense peace over it, I don't receive it. I'll ask the Lord in the moment, is this from You? He always answers because He wants to speak to us, and He does not want us to be deceived.

We should always encourage others when giving a word. For example, if God shows you that a person is living in a place of sin, but you also see that the chains are falling off of them in their future, you could say something like, the Lord sees that you are having a difficult time right now, but He wants you to know that your chains are being broken off right now. I see that you are becoming free. You have just validated their life without embarrassing them, and you've spoken life and hope into them.

### Proverbs 18:21 (NKJV)
<sup></sup>21 Death and life are in the power of the tongue,
And those who love it will eat its fruit.

With God at your side and His love as your motive, you can never do harm encouraging others. Be attentive to your Father's voice. You may be the only encouraging word someone has received in years.

I'm reminded of a story of two long-time friends who had lost touch for many years. For purposes of this story, I will call them Kathy and Lauren. Kathy and Lauren were catching up over the phone. Lauren was sharing about the many losses she had endured through the years. She had not been attending church anymore and even questioned God's love and character. At the end of the phone call, Kathy asked if she could pray for her. Lauren replied yes. As Kathy prayed, Lauren began crying. As they were getting ready to hang up, Lauren still crying said, "No one has prayed for me in ten years." She continued to cry. It pierced Kathy's heart. She had no idea the power and encouragement of a simple prayer.

You might be the only connection for someone else to God today. Go out and share the love of Jesus with everyone you see. Be a blessing to others just because you can.

# *Journaling Questions*

1. Lord, is it okay to receive an encouraging word from You for someone else?
2. Lord, show me where You have been speaking to me and I was not listening.
3. Lord, show me where I have specifically heard Your voice and how it positively benefitted my life.
4. Lord, how do I encourage someone if You show me something negative?
5. What am I supposed to do with negative information that You show me?
6. What else do You want me to know today?

# Notes

# Chapter Eight

# Discernment

In Webster's Dictionary, discernment is:

1.   The quality of being able to grasp and comprehend what is obscure: skill in discerning;
2.   An act of perceiving or discerning something.

The gift of discerning of spirits is different than discernment. Everyone has a level of discernment that they operate in. Discernment is the ability to perceive things in the natural. Natural discernment employs deduction and wisdom. The gift of discerning of spirits is the supernatural ability to perceive what's going on in the atmosphere. This gift is a supernatural gift that the Lord gives to believers.

Here's an example of natural discernment: You're at a Christmas party, and you are talking to a group of people. You notice in the conversation that one person in particular seems to know a lot of personal information about many people, and they don't mind sharing it with others. Natural discernment tells you to be careful what you say around that person because it will probably be repeated.

Here's an example of the gift of discerning of Spirits:

**Acts 16:16–18 (NKJV)**
16 Now it happened, as we went to prayer, that a certain slave girl possessed with a spirit of divination met us, who brought her masters much profit by fortune-telling. 17 This girl followed Paul and us, and cried out, saying, "These men are the servants of the Most High God, who proclaim to us the way of salvation." 18 And this she did for many days. But Paul, greatly annoyed, turned and said to the spirit, "I command you in the name of Jesus Christ to come out from her." And he came out that very hour.

Paul was operating in the gift of discerning of Spirits. What the slave girl said was accurate; however, the motivation behind it was demonic. Paul discerned this from the Lord. He then took authority over the spirit and commanded it to come out.

The gift of discerning of spirits is supernatural and is for the purpose of discerning what's going on around you in the spirit. There are four different spirits that this gift will discern: the presence of God, the presence of angels, the presence of demons, and the heart and/or motive of a person's spirit.

Another interesting thing about this gift is that you may be discerning something in the atmosphere while the person sitting right next to you may not notice anything. (2 Kings 6:15–17) This is one of the reasons that this gift is so important—a person operating in this gift might see what others may not see.

This is my story and lesson that I was taught about the gift of discerning of spirits years ago. It is an extreme lesson, but I think God wanted to make sure that I understood.

I was in my early thirties at the time. I had been a Christian for fifteen years at this point, and I had just been baptized in the Holy Spirit. The Lord was opening up a realm of the supernatural that I was totally unaware of at this point in my life. Of course you hear stories, but nothing had hit home until this night.

I met with a group of women from church at a local restaurant. We all had a nice dinner and great fellowship. At the end of the evening, everyone had pretty much left. There was one person still there besides me. We discussed some prayer requests, and we decided to pray for them before we both left. The restaurant was closed; so we went out to my vehicle, which was parked in front of the restaurant, and began to pray.

It was late, 11:00 o'clock or so in the evening. So as we were sitting in my car, we closed our eyes, and my friend began to pray. I instantly began to sense something was wrong. My friend said, just press in. She was totally in the Spirit and praying. I was sitting there like a German shepherd on patrol. I told her that something was wrong. She looked at me and instantly, we both jumped out of the car, thinking that someone might be in the car. We checked everywhere, and the car was empty. It was just the two of us present.

We got back in, locked the doors and returned to pray. Again, I was still sensing that something was not right. She continued to say, "Just press in." She was aggravated with me, and I was aggravated with her. I knew in my spirit that something was off, but I didn't know what it was. All of a sudden, two police cars came driving into the parking lot two cars away from us with lights flashing and sirens. We looked over, still in our locked vehicle, and the police had a man in their custody. They put him up against the car, handcuffed him, and removed a gun from him. They proceeded to put him in the squad car, and then they drove away.

My friend just looked at me. We talked for a few minutes about it and then went back to praying again. We both thought that everything was safe and sound. My friend closed her eyes to pray. I began sensing something again—even stronger. At this point, she was getting extremely annoyed with me because she was not sensing anything at all. All of a sudden, a limousine drove up and parked two lanes away from us. A man got out of the front of the vehicle and opened the passenger door. He dragged a female out of the vehicle and proceeded to start hitting her there in the parking lot. I heard the Lord clearly say, "Get out of there now!" My friend looked at me and said, "I heard it, too."

I drove my friend back to her car, and we both left. The police showed up again. My heart was pounding on the drive home. I had sensed the presence of evil both times. My friend, who had different gifts, was not discerning the presence of evil.

Many times in my life, people had called me paranoid, when actually God was speaking to me and I didn't recognize His voice. Weeks before this experience, I had asked the Lord why I had this gift. I didn't see the practical use for it. I saw how others operated in their spiritual gifts. I just didn't understand; this was all new to me. I look back at that moment now and laugh for a multitude of reasons, but God is so faithful to answer our prayers. It just may not be the way you expect Him to answer.

First Corinthians 12 speaks of us all being a part of one body. If we were all the hands, who would communicate or give instruction as to where we serve?

If you don't know what your spiritual gifts are, ask your church. Many churches have spiritual gift tests that they use to educate their people so that they can be trained and equipped for the body of Christ. Once you have determined what your gifts are, educate yourself about your specific gifts. Find out the good, the bad, and the ugly of those gifts. You'll be amazed at what you will learn. It will give you a new understanding of why and how you may do certain things and also why you're so passionate about other things.

Don and Katie Fortune have a great book called "Discover your Children's Gifts."[1] This book has so much information in it. It made an impact in how we made certain decisions while raising our children. We were able to tell, for the most part, the gifts of each of our children at a very young age as a result of reading this book. Our parenting style changed a little to help encourage them in their different gifts. As they got older and took the tests for themselves, we found that the tests from this book were spot-on in identifying our children's gifts. It not only helped us with our children, but it also gave us insight into other people who had the same or similar gifts.

First Corinthians 14 says that the spiritual gifts are given for the edification (encouragement) of the church. They are not to boast of oneself, and they are certainly not to be used to manipulate, control, or judge others.

I want to stop right here for a moment: if you are reading this and a pastor, teacher, or Christian has used these gifts against you; I apologize to you. I am so sorry for any misuse of God's gifts. The gift of discerning of spirits does not give us the right to judge others. The Bible is specific:

**Matthew 7:1–2 (NKJV)**
7 "Judge not, that you be not judged. 2 For with what judgment you judge, you will be judged, and with the measure you use, it will be measured back to you.

There are times, if you have this gift, that you will see the sin in someone's heart or you will see an attitude or a motive. This information is given to you supernaturally, and it must be guarded and used wisely. Most importantly, information from God about someone else should always be used in love. Without love, we are a clanging cymbal (1 Corinthians 13:1).

Sometimes God will show you something to protect you or others, but most of the time, God is showing you this so that you can pray for that person in private. He's not calling on you to be the junior Holy Spirit and call that person out. He wants you to be a person of prayer and of great love. Love restores people; it does not humiliate or hurt them.

I love the story of Jesus restoring Peter. Peter denied Jesus three times, and Jesus, being so full of love, restored him through a question asked three times. He didn't tell Peter all of the things that He discerned about him. He publicly restored him with such amazing love that Peter became one of the greatest evangelists of all times.

Love should always be our motive. If you feel you don't have enough love—Guess what? You're right. You don't; however, Jesus has all of the love that you need. Ask Him to give you His heart, His eyes—His love…

### 1 Corinthians 12:12–18 (NKJV)

12 For as the body is one and has many members, but all the members of that one body, being many, are one body, so also is Christ. 13 For by one Spirit we were all baptized into one body—whether Jews or Greeks, whether slaves or free—and have all been made to drink into one Spirit. 14 For in fact the body is not one member but many.

15 If the foot should say, "Because I am not a hand, I am not of the body," is it therefore not of the body? 16 And if the ear should say, "Because I am not an eye, I am not of the body," is it therefore not of the body? 17 If the whole body were an eye, where would be the hearing? If the whole were hearing, where would be the smelling? 18 But now God has

set the members, each one of them, in the body just
as He pleased.

I believe that when we, as Christians, know our identity in
Christ, we will walk in the gifts that God has given us, and we
will stop comparing ourselves to other people and their gifts.
We can then begin to walk together in unity, and the unity of
the body of Christ will change the atmosphere spiritually in
our lives, in our homes, in our churches, in our cities, and in
our nation. Then we can make an impact world-wide.

Just be who you are in Christ. If the Lord, who created you,
thought it was good, maybe you should, too. When you embrace the gifts that God has given you, you can relax and enjoy
life a little more because you trust His gifts to supernaturally
manifest within you when you need them. We must walk being aware of the Holy Spirit's presence upon us. These gifts
are not our ability and we can never take credit for them. All
glory, honor, and praise go to the King of Kings and Lord of
Lords.

The gift of discerning of spirits is a wonderful gift. Another
aspect of this gift is the supernatural ability to perceive the
presence of God or angels in a room. I love that you can sense
His presence. When He walks into the room, the atmosphere
changes. It is in His presence that lives are changed.

No matter what type of ministry you're involved in, the gift
of discerning of spirits can be very helpful. In ministry, you
may see, in the Spirit, a demonic presence or influence around
a person. According to the information that you've been giv-
en (supernaturally), you can pray accordingly. Command the
spirit to leave in Jesus' name and then pursue healing. Don't
put so much focus on the demonic, but rather when it gets in
the way, take authority over it and then continue on the path
you're walking. Satan is defeated! Jesus made a public specta-
cle of him. All authority was given to us through Jesus. Don't

go looking for demons, but when you discern their presence, take authority over them and continue on your walk. Remember the ditches I spoke about earlier? Be careful not to fall in. Jesus didn't go looking for demons. They were brought to Him. He cast them out. He healed the people and their lives were restored. This is our commission:

### Matthew 10:7–8 (NKJV)

[7] And as you go, preach, saying, 'The kingdom of heaven is at hand.' [8] Heal the sick, cleanse the lepers, raise the dead, cast out demons. Freely you have received, freely give.

Here's another example of how this gift works regarding other people: Years ago, I attended a funeral service for someone that had attended our church. At the funeral, the person giving the eulogy was speaking about the deceased. I continued to listen to the speaker, and I noticed that they were really building this person up above and beyond a normal funeral service. I was young in the Lord at the time. As I listened, I began to feel very uncomfortable. I knew in my spirit that something was off, but I did not know what it was. The feeling in me was getting so strong that I wanted to get up and leave. I did not want to be disrespectful, so I stayed. Later, I spoke to my pastor about it, and he explained what was going on. He confirmed that I was discerning something even though I didn't know what it was.

Always surround yourself with Godly, mature believers. Don't think that you have to know everything. When something comes up that you don't understand, take it to those that are mature in Christ so that they can help you to understand. As you learn to hear the Lord's voice, you can ask Him all of these things; however, don't forget about your mentors or your accountability partner. Confirm with them that you are hearing correctly.

Remember that when you receive a word from the Lord, there are some characteristics that must lie within that content. Does the word line up with the Word of God? Does it reflect the character of God? Will the word bring forth good fruit? Is it given in love? If not—go back and try again. It's okay if you miss it initially—you're learning. The more you step out and journal, the more you will recognize His voice. You will be able to tell if it's your voice, God's voice or Satan's voice.

### James 3:13–18 (NKJV)
### Heavenly Versus Demonic Wisdom

[13] Who is wise and understanding among you? Let him show by good conduct that his works are done in the meekness of wisdom. [14] But if you have bitter envy and self-seeking in your hearts, do not boast and lie against the truth. [15] This wisdom does not descend from above, but is earthly, sensual, demonic. [16] For where envy and self-seeking exist, confusion and every evil thing are there. [17] But the wisdom that is from above is first pure, then peaceable, gentle, willing to yield, full of mercy and good fruits, without partiality and without hypocrisy. [18] Now the fruit of righteousness is sown in peace by those who make peace.

In our small group, we encourage people to listen, discern, and speak a word from the Lord. The biggest fear of everyone is: what if I missed it? It's okay as you are learning to hone in on the voice of God. Practice with people that you feel safe with, not those that would condemn and judge you.

When a child begins to take his first steps, what happens after a few steps? He falls. Do you condemn him for falling? Do you say, "What's wrong with you? You should know how to walk." Of course you wouldn't say that to your child. What do you do? You walk over to him, stand him up, take a few steps backward and encourage him to try again. You encourage him—come on, you can do it. Come to me.

Let's do that with one another. Let's encourage one another to come to God. Let us be people of God that are known for their love and encouragement. After all, Love is the greatest gift.

# *Journaling Questions*

1. Where were You trying to communicate to me through the gift of discerning of spirits and I did not see it?
2. How have You protected me in my life as a result of this gift?
3. What is the purpose of this gift in my life?
4. Is there any place that I have misused this gift?
5. What else do You want me to know about natural discernment and spiritual discernment?

# Notes

# Chapter Nine

# Obstacles to Hearing

*Balance and Accountability*

Just as everything in life should be balanced, so should the teaching on hearing and recognizing God's voice. I want to share a few warnings that I have learned through the years. These are my lessons that I am sharing with you now. I hope that you will take the meat and leave the bones.

*Life Experiences*

The first thing I want to talk about is life experiences. We must be careful to not allow life experiences to hinder us from hearing God's voice. Let me explain what I mean. Let's look at the story of Job. There are many incredible teachings that come from this story; however, what I want to focus on is one statement he made in Job 3:25, (NKJV) *"For the thing I greatly feared has come upon me, And what I dreaded has happened to me."*

Job's life experience had taught him that these things would happen to him because he had seen or heard of it in his life or the lives of others up to this point. He also feared what he had seen and/or experienced in life.

So for practical purposes, let's say that I am praying for the salvation of a family member. I watch as that member lives a worldly lifestyle. I also listen to other friends, acquaintances, friends at church, and others who tell me of their family members who have wandered in the desert for forty or fifty years without accepting Christ. I hear from others that a family member died and never received Jesus as their personal Savior. So life experience has spoken and shown me that it may not happen or probably won't happen, and that I will never see them again. So now I'm journaling and the Lord gives me a *Rhema* (spoken) word saying that this person will turn his or her heart to the Lord. The Lord gives me words of knowledge about this person and speaks prophetic words about their future as well. He also gives me scriptures from the Bible to back up what He is saying. In the moment that the Lord gives me the word, I receive it, but as days go by, I begin to see the person or the situation in the natural and the words from the Spirit of God seem less likely to be true. Even though I know that God does not lie, negative thoughts start to flood my mind. What if I missed it? What if that was my voice—my own desire—because I wanted it so bad? What do I do? Then fear sets in. All of a sudden, Job 3:25 comes—the thing that I greatly feared has come upon me.

Fear will immobilize you. The acronym for F.E.A.R. is False Evidence Appearing Real. Regardless of what life experience has taught us, regardless of what we have seen or heard; our default or auto response must always be Jesus and what He said.

When this happens, stand on the Word of God. God's Word is infallible. If you cannot trust that you are hearing correctly, go back to the Word of God and ask for His Word to give you strength and comfort. God will always answer you. He loves you. He sees your pain. He wants to talk to you.

Jesus is the Word, and He is life. The Bible is the living Word inspired by the breath of the Holy Spirit. The Bible, the Word, is life to those who believe. (Hebrews 4:12)

### Balance

If you are living on the side of receiving *Rhema* words (spoken) from the Lord only without reading the *Logos* (written) Word of God, the Bible, then you are out of balance. On the other hand, if you are only reading the Word of God and not hearing or recognizing how God is speaking to you in other ways, you, too, are out of balance.

Remember the ditches—don't fall in. Please hear my heart. I am not judging you for being on either side. These have been my lessons to learn for I have been in both ditches at times. God's desire for me is to be in balance, and that is God's best for my life and yours.

Can God supernaturally download the Word of God within us? Yes, of course He could; however, I believe that the Lord enjoys watching our journey of discovering new things, seeing us receive new revelation from Him. It's the day-to-day time spent with Him in the Word that we begin to truly know the character of God. The Holy Spirit will bring to your remembrance -- If the Holy Spirit is going to do His part—bring it to your remembrance—then we must do our part by reading the Word so that He can recall it to our mind. Does that make sense?

**John 14:26 (NKJV)**
26 But the Helper, the Holy Spirit, whom the Father will send in My name, He will teach you all things, and bring to your remembrance all things that I said to you.

*Emotionally Stirred*

Sometimes we are so emotionally stirred that it becomes difficult to hear clearly, to determine if these are my thoughts or His thoughts. When this happens to me, I call upon two or three mature believers to confirm one way or the other what I'm hearing. Let me interject right here that if you don't have one or two accountability partners—get one! Having no accountability in your life is also a ditch. Accountability protects you. In my opinion, it cannot only be your spouse. If that's all you have for a season, then that is what you have, but if you are going through life without having any other relationships or accountability, you're in a ditch. Climb out. Life is about relationships and community. Jesus has set the example. He is and has always been in relationship with the Father and the Holy Spirit. He wants a relationship with the ones that He created, and He wants us to have relationships with others.

If I'm really struggling with what I'm hearing, I will call an accountability partner and ask them to pray for me. I'll tell them what I'm hearing, and if I've chosen that person well, they will be honest with me. I don't know about you, but for me, I need a pit bull for an accountability partner. It will not help me to grow in Christ if I partner with someone that just says yes to me or agrees with me all the time. I need to be challenged in love. If I don't agree with what they said, I'll go back to the Lord and pray about it. I'll read His Word and seek Him. He always seems to get His message to me. I trust the Lord to speak to me, and He always does.

*Bad Teaching*

Sometimes bad Christian teaching will affect your hearing or the way that you recognize God's voice. For example, if you've been taught that God gives and God takes away, (which, by the way, is not stated in the Bible like that at all) then you will believe that God is a ruler with an iron fist who looks for opportunities to punish you, to take things away from you. Isn't that contrary to the word of God?

**Matthew 7:11 (NKJV)**
If you then, being evil, know how to give good gifts to your children, how much more will your Father who is in heaven give good things to those who ask Him!

✧   ✧   ✧

**James 1:16–17 (NKJV)**
16 Do not be deceived, my beloved brethren. 17 Every good gift and every perfect gift is from above, and comes down from the Father of lights, with whom there is no variation or shadow of turning.

This is an example of bad teaching: If you hear something from the Lord while journaling that says that He wants to bless you, His desire is that you prosper. Your inheritance through Jesus Christ is to be blessed. So if you believe that God gives and takes away, you'll be waiting for the shoe to drop, and there will be doubt present. So your belief system is already tainted. Your belief is that the Creator of the Universe, who created you, just wants to give you something good so that He can take it away. That's really silly when you think about it. What has happened is that the character of God has been tainted by bad teaching or life's circumstances. This is why we must read the Bible and know the Word—not for head knowledge, but to know the heart of God. He is good! He is loving! He is kind! He is generous! He has your best interest at heart! Satan is the one who comes to steal, kill and destroy.

> John 10:10 (NKJV) The thief does not come except to steal, and to kill, and to destroy. I have come that they may have life, and that they may have it more abundantly.

When we know the character of God, we will begin to see the amazing love that He has for us. When we know who He is and who we are in Him, we will no longer live in fear of a mean God. I'm not talking about having a reverential fear of God—that's different. I'm talking about knowing, really knowing that God is good and He desires the best for you. He desires to bless you because He loves you! He loves you! If you hear nothing else today, know that your Heavenly Father loves you.

### Unforgiveness

The above sections are some of the reasons that hearing or recognizing God's voice may be hindered, but I cannot close this chapter without mentioning unforgiveness.

Unforgiveness affects us in many ways, but for me personally, it's like turning off the faucet so that no water can drip down. When I have unforgiveness in my heart, I don't even want to talk to the Lord. Why? Because I think I already know what He's going to tell me—you know, He'll use scripture on me (Ha Ha!).

Yet, He never ceases to amaze me! When I'm living with unforgiveness and I finally say, "Okay, Lord, I'm ready to hear you," He speaks to me with such love. He seems to validate my hurt and yet His love draws me to repentance. He is so *amazing*. As soon as I truly repent in my heart, it's like the faucet has been turned on full blast. The flow is continuous from Him. If I choose not to forgive; I am the one that shuts off the flow of the river of Life.

So if there is any unforgiveness in your life, take it to Jesus. He'll work through it with you. He loves you! He cares about every detail of your life. Surrender your pain, your hurt, and your unforgiveness to Him. I promise, He will heal you, re-store you, and lift you up. God has so much for you. Don't let unforgiveness stop the flow.

# *Journaling Questions*

1.  Lord, show me where I have allowed unforgiveness in my life.
2.  Lord, is there any place in my life that I'm out of balance? And if so, what can I do to correct this?
3.  Who do You suggest would be a good accountability partner for me?
4.  What else do You want me to know today?

# Notes

# Chapter Ten

# Desensitization

Desensitization, according to Webster's Dictionary:

1. To make (a sensitized or hypersensitive individual) insensitive or nonreactive to a sensitizing agent;
2. To make emotionally insensitive or callous; specifically: to extinguish an emotional response (as of fear, anxiety, or guilt) to stimuli that formerly induced it.

In basic training of new recruits for the armed services, one of the main tactics of Drill Sergeants is to desensitize the recruits. The first three months of boot camp is a lot of physical and emotional preparation. They want them to become less reactive to their surroundings and reliant upon the one voice that they hear. What are they trying to accomplish? Actually quite a few things, but one specific goal is to get them to not feel fear, anxiety, and the like, and also to be desensitized to pain and suffering. Why is this important? It enables them to carry out the orders of the Commander, especially if it is a difficult task that would, for the average person, be emotionally too difficult to carry out. The recruit is trained to listen to the voice of the Commander and follow the instructions given to a tee. I am grateful for the men and women who serve in our armed services. They truly give up a lot for the protection of the people of the United States of America. We bless them.

I believe that we are all desensitized to some degree; however, we can change that, if we desire. Let me give you a couple of examples:

How many times have you been trying to have a conversation with someone, their phone buzzes, and they pick it up in the middle of your conversation to text someone else. After a while of being desensitized by others in this, I have actually caught myself doing this. I have to be conscious of "actually being with" the person I am with at the time. I am retraining myself to not "look at it." The cell phone distracts me from the conversation that I am having, and it communicates to the other person that they are not as important as that text or phone call. We have become so dependent on our fast fix of communication that we are not interested in anything that takes time.

When my grandmother was alive, I remember going to her house, and she would always have a puzzle set up on a coffee table. When family or other people came in, they could just sit for a few minutes and work at putting the puzzle pieces together. It was actually relaxing. She was a smart woman. Looking back, what she had done was to provide an opportunity for conversation over a puzzle.

My grandfather and I used to play cards. We spent hours together playing cards and talking. I know that the days are different, but now I play solitaire on my iPad. Do you see what I'm saying? I'm actually content playing a computer game by myself as opposed to asking someone to sit at the table and play cards. I have been desensitized so that I am content being by myself playing a game of cards instead of continuing to build relationships. Don't get me wrong, I love some of the technology, but it shouldn't replace quality time with people. Technology has a lot of positives, and I am grateful for it. So for all of you techies, relax. I'm not picking on the technologies. I'm simply trying to make a point—we have been desensitized in the smallest things without realizing it.

Just like boot camp, there is an enemy who is attempting to train us to become less sensitive to the things of God. He uses the resources of the world to do it—through media, technology, television, music, gaming, and many other ways. What is his goal? Satan does not want us to listen to the voice of God, much less be obedient to His voice.

Desensitization can also make us not desire the things of God. If I watch, for example, four episodes of a show that is tense and violent; it's going to be hard for me to turn the TV off and flip on worship music and get in the presence of God. Maybe it's not hard for you, but it is for me. I have to throw off the things of this world—the thoughts, negative or otherwise, the four episodes, and try to set my mind on things above. I will probably have to put on quite a bit of praise music before I can even think of entering into worship. At this point, it will be a process going from the outer courts to the inner courts and into the Holy of Holies—the presence of God. Why? Because my heart was not sensitive to the Lord.

Each of us have things in our lives that may keep us from hearing the voice of God. This is not a guilt message for any of us. I'm not saying that I don't watch movies because I do. I live in a house of men. When they watch a movie, they want something to blow up in the first five minutes or they've lost interest. Their idea of a chick-flick is a female blowing something up in the first five minutes. All I'm saying is: be sensitive to the Holy Spirit. He'll direct you in all your ways.

How do we become sensitive to God and His Kingdom purposes? Get into the presence of God. He is the One who renews our minds. He is the One who can take a desensitized heart and make it hypersensitive to Him. We just need to come to Him, be hungry for Him.

> **Ezekiel 36:26 (NKJV)**
> I will give you a new heart and put a new spirit within you; I will take the heart of stone out of your flesh and give you a heart of flesh.

Now that we're aware of this tactic of the enemy, let's purpose in our hearts to be sensitive to the Holy Spirit. Let's purpose to hear the Lord's voice. Let's purpose to fulfill our destiny in Christ Jesus and not allow the enemy's tactic to derail our destiny.

# *Journaling Questions*

1.  Lord, what do You want me to know about desensitization?
2.  Lord, in what areas of my life have I allowed the enemy to desensitize me to Your voice and to Your ways?
3.  Lord, what are some practical ways that I can change this?
4.  What else do You want to speak to me about today?

# Notes

# Chapter Eleven

# Deception

This is a tough subject because as Christians, we do not want to think that we can be deceived. The Bible warns us of deception. How does a person fall into deception? It begins with a seed—a thought that is sown into your heart and mind. Depending on what you do with the thought, you will set into motion a positive or negative response.

> **Romans 16:17–18 (NKJV)**
> [17] Now I urge you, brethren, note those who cause divisions and offenses, contrary to the doctrine which you learned, and avoid them. [18] For those who are such do not serve our Lord Jesus Christ, but their own belly, and by smooth words and flattering speech deceive the hearts of the simple.

The Greek word for "deceive" in Romans 16:18 means to seduce wholly, beguile. It's the same word used in 1 Corinthians 3:18.

> **1 Corinthians 3:18–20 (NKJV)**
> [18] Let no one deceive himself. If anyone among you seems to be wise in this age, let him become a fool that he may become wise. [19] For the wisdom of this

world is foolishness with God. For it is written, "He catches the wise in their own craftiness"; [20] and again, "the Lord knows the thoughts of the wise, that they are futile."

Let me give you an example: Let's say there is a couple that has been married for ten years. The pressures of life have put a demand on the couple to work longer hours so that they can produce the income necessary for their home. After a while, they aren't spending as much time together. They aren't attending church regularly. They're not spending time in the Word. They are not spending time with the Lord; however, they are spending more time with friends at work. There's more tension in the home.

The enemy begins to whisper things about the other person. "He doesn't appreciate what I do for him. She doesn't appreciate anything that I do for her." Compliments and encouraging words for one another have now turned into biting remarks and criticism. Now all of a sudden, the woman is at work, and a coworker begins to compliment how nice she looks. He takes her to lunch, opens the door to the restaurant for her, pulls her chair out for her as she sits, and insists on paying. Thoughts begin to enter her mind, such as "I wish my husband treated me like this. This guy is such a gentleman. He is this ... He is that ... My husband this ... My husband that ..." And before you know it, she is having an affair, and she did not see it coming. If you asked her about it, she could probably rationalize why this is the right thing for her to do. Did she plan on having an affair? No, but she did not guard her thought life. She was deceived.

**1 Peter 5:8 (NKJV)**
[8] Be sober, be vigilant; because your adversary the devil walks about like a roaring lion, seeking whom he may devour.

✧ ✧ ✧

**2 Corinthians 10:4–5 (NKJV)**
[4] For the weapons of our warfare are not carnal but mighty in God for pulling down strongholds, [5] casting down arguments and every high thing that exalts itself against the knowledge of God, bringing every thought into captivity to the obedience of Christ.

Deception begins with a thought. This is why we must daily renew our minds in Christ. The more that we feast on the Word of God, the more we know Him. The more that we linger in His presence; the more we learn how to host His presence everywhere we go. When we focus more on God and His kingdom, His passion will become our passion.

The world is fighting for our attention. There are distractions everywhere. If I want to believe God for something to happen or to take place in my life; then I must focus on the Words that He has promised me. Let me give you an example: If you believe God that your prodigal child will come back to the Lord; then you must stand on His Word. Find every scripture that you can about what the Bible tells you about raising your child, God's plan for your child, and anything else related to your situation. Take those scriptures, type them up and post a copy of it somewhere that you will see every day. Read those scriptures out loud and declare them over your child. What happens? The Word of God is life. It begins to stir your spirit, and faith grows within you. You begin to be encouraged by those words.

What has God told you specifically about your child? Is he or she an evangelist, a teacher, or a preacher? Then declare His *Rhema* words over that child. This is how we take our thoughts captive according to 2 Corinthians 10:5. Remember what God has spoken about your son or daughter. Believe the Lord and the words that He has spoken. They will carry you through that season. We cannot give up and allow our thoughts to defeat us. Eternity with Christ is the only option. Pray, declare, and stand with the same intensity of the need. God loves that kind of faith and fervency. He will show up and show up *big*!

If you don't stand on the Word of God, you may become tempted to be discouraged or feel like your situation is hopeless. Build yourself up. Stay full of the Word of God. Encourage yourself. You'll find that as you are encouraged by Him, you will be able to encourage others who are also going through the same situation.

It does not matter what situation you are going through in life; God is with you and His wisdom is available to you. There is not a situation in life that you are facing that you cannot find counsel from the Word of God. If you need healing, then find scriptures about healing. If you are dealing with lack, find out what the Bible says about finances. If you need relationship help, find out what the Word of God says about relationships. Allow the Word of God to bring hope to your circumstances. Whatever your situation is, find the scriptures that you need to carry you through the season of life that you're in. Read them, memorize them, and declare them over your life. Meditate on them. And when you've done all of those things— stand in faith, with assurance that your Father in heaven has heard your prayers and is already moving mountains on your behalf. He loves you so much.

Know today that you are not alone. We all struggle at one point or another. That's why we need each other. No one except Jesus has it altogether. Take captive every thought from the enemy. Replace those thoughts by meditating on things above.

**Philippians 4:8 (NKJV)**
⁸ Finally, brethren, whatever things are true, whatever things are noble, whatever things are just, whatever things are pure, whatever things are lovely, whatever things are of good report, if there is any virtue and if there is anything praiseworthy—meditate on these things.

✿  ✿  ✿

**Romans 12:2 (NKJV)**
² And do not be conformed to this world, but be transformed by the renewing of your mind, that you may prove what is that good and acceptable and perfect will of God.

My family likes Sci-fi—not the weird or horror type, but entertaining Sci-fi. Anyways, I remember a time when we were watching a lot of the series, *Stargate SG-1*. We couldn't wait for the next season to come out. We thought about it, talked about it, and anticipated the day that the new release would come out. Well, it was Christmas Eve one year, and we attended a local church's Christmas Eve service. They had beautiful Christmas decorations all over the church. Right in the middle of the stage, they had made a very large circular ring which sat on the stage. They used a projection machine to show videos through it. Now, if you've seen *Stargate*, you already know what I'm talking about. One of my boys leaned over next to me and just about the same time we said, "Hey, look at the Stargate." We just chuckled together. However, I kept looking at the design (while the service was going on, I might add), and I was totally distracted by the ring. Obviously, I was watching too much *Stargate*. I think you would agree that I needed to renew my mind on the things above, not on a science fiction show. Whatever we focus on, our thought life and our words will flow from it.

**Luke 6:45 (NKJV)**
A good man out of the good treasure of his heart brings forth good, and an evil man out of the evil treasure of his heart brings forth evil. For out of the abundance of the heart his mouth speaks.

We are all tempted at times to take into our heart the lies that are presented to us on a daily basis. This is why it is important to know the Lord's voice so that when a thought comes from the enemy, we will recognize it and cast it down.

How does the enemy deceive us? Through lies which start with a thought.

**Genesis 20 (NKJV)**
20 And Abraham journeyed from there to the South, and dwelt between Kadesh and Shur, and stayed in Gerar. 2 Now Abraham said of Sarah his wife, "She is my sister." And Abimelech king of Gerar sent and took Sarah. 3 But God came to Abimelech in a dream by night, and said to him, "Indeed you are a dead man because of the woman whom you have taken, for she is a man's wife."
4 But Abimelech had not come near her, and he said, "Lord, will You slay a righteous nation also? 5 Did he not say to me, 'She is my sister'? And she, even she herself said, 'He is my brother.' In the integrity of my heart and innocence of my hands I have done this." 6 And God said to him in a dream, "Yes, I know that you did this in the integrity of your heart. For I also withheld you from sinning against Me; therefore I did not let you touch her. 7 Now therefore, restore the man's wife; for he is a

prophet, and he will pray for you and you shall live. But if you do not restore her, know that you shall surely die, you and all who are yours." ⁸ So Abimelech rose early in the morning, called all his servants, and told all these things in their hearing, and the men were very much afraid. ⁹ And Abimelech called Abraham and said to him, "What have you done to us? How have I offended you, that you have brought on me and on my kingdom a great sin? You have done deeds to me that ought not to be done." ¹⁰ Then Abimelech said to Abraham, "What did you have in view, that you have done this thing?"

¹¹ And Abraham said, "Because I thought, surely the fear of God is not in this place, and they will kill me on account of my wife. ¹² But indeed she is truly my sister. She is the daughter of my father, but not the daughter of my mother, and she became my wife. ¹³ And it came to pass, when God caused me to wander from my father's house, that I said to her, 'This is your kindness that you should do for me: in every place, wherever we go, say of me, "He is my brother."'" ¹⁴ Then Abimelech took sheep, oxen, and male and female servants, and gave them to Abraham, and he restored Sarah his wife to him. ¹⁵ And Abimelech said, "See, my land is before you; dwell where it pleases you." ¹⁶ Then to Sarah he said, "Behold, I have given your brother a thousand pieces of silver; indeed this vindicates you before all who are with you and before everybody." Thus she was rebuked. ¹⁷ So Abraham prayed to God, and God healed Abimelech, his wife, and his female servants. Then they bore children; ¹⁸ for the Lord had closed up all the wombs of the house of Abimelech because of Sarah, Abraham's wife.

The thought came to Abraham—"They will kill me on account of my wife." Fear began to set in. He began to believe that if they knew Sarah was his wife, they would kill him. So Abraham's solution was to lie about Sarah—saying that she was his sister. His behavior changed to support the lie. He now allowed his wife to be taken by another man. Of course, God intervened and made things right. Do you see how we can live our life based on the lies or the truth that we believe? It's interesting that Isaac six chapters later repeats the same behavior. Isaac believed the same lie. Again, God intervened.

If you believe the lies of the enemy, they will take root and become part of your belief system. As life goes on, the enemy will continue to feed those lies and make them grow and take on more lies.

For example, a person who has grown up hearing these types of words—"You'll never amount to anything, you're stupid, and so on," will at some point begin to believe that they are stupid and they will never amount to anything in this life. Then their behavior begins to line up with those words until that core belief is established in their life. Then one day someone tries to show them how to do something another way, and their instant response is: "I know what I'm doing. I'm not an idiot." Where does that come from? The root goes back to the words that were spoken to them or over them throughout their life, and now those words (lies) have power over that person. Deception becomes a way of life.

The Holy Spirit is the only person that can break deception off of a person. Multiple people can tell the person that they're not stupid and that they did not mean it that way, but if that seed—that lie, is still there and it feels true to them, they will not believe what you are telling them. When a person is deceived, they just don't see it.

**Luke 3:9 (NKJV)**
⁹ And even now the axe is laid to the root of the trees. Therefore every tree which does not bear good fruit is cut down and thrown into the fire.

If something in your life is not producing the fruit spoken of in Galatians 5:22–23, then ask the Lord to help you take an axe to the root. God's desire is for us to be free. If we ask Him to put His finger on any and all deception in our lives, He will do it. One of the many things I love about the Lord is that He always provides a way for us. He is a Great and Mighty God!

# *Journaling Questions*

1. What are the lies that I believe in my life?
2. Jesus, if the lie is: _____
   (fill in your lie), what do You say is the truth?

Go through each lie individually with the Lord. It does not matter whether there is one lie or fifteen; ask the Lord to replace each lie with His truth. Make the time; it will be well worth your effort.

Prayer: Jesus, fill every empty place in me where the enemy has held me captive. I desire more of You in my life. I love You, Lord!

# Notes

# Chapter Twelve

# Prayer

Prayer is communication with God. Simply put, prayer is just talking to God. We talk to other people every day. God wants us to spend time with Him each day as well. God is not religious; so we don't have to speak in "King Jameth" speech to impress Him. Speak to Him like you would anyone else.

By the way, when you hear His voice, for the most part, it will be similar to the way that you speak. I am not a King James Version user, so I am not going to hear scriptures or words from the Lord in that form.

When I pray or talk to God, I pray from my heart. It may not sound profound or flowery, but it is my heart. I know that my Daddy loves to hear my voice, my words. He loves how I come to Him. He created me, and He created me uniquely. You are also unique. The way that you approach your Heavenly Father will sound different from the way that I approach Him. He loves to hear your voice! He loves you as you are— just you! God desires to talk to you. Talk to Him like a friend. He is your friend, and He will understand you.

There are different types of prayer. Journaling is one type of prayer. It's, in my opinion, the best kind of two-way prayer— you speak to God and He responds back to you. Journaling on paper will help you develop a natural lifestyle of prayer or two-way communication with the Lord.

Intercessory prayer is another type of prayer. Intercession is when we pray for other people. When we intercede, we go before the Lord on their behalf.

Fasting with prayer is also a type of prayer. I find that my spiritual senses seem to be heightened when I am fasting. Fasting is a surrendering of your will and your desires to draw closer to God. Some of the benefits of fasting are receiving God's wisdom and revelation in your life, answered prayer, and many other things.

Praying in the Spirit is another type of prayer. With a limited vocabulary to pray for others, our prayer language allows the Holy Spirit to pray through us. When the Holy Spirit prays, He is praying a perfect prayer because He is perfect.

Regardless of what type of prayer we are using, it brings us into a closer relationship with the Lord. Prayer draws us into a deeper place. Effective prayer requires speaking to God, listening to what He has to say and then obeying Him.

### Fasting

One thing that I have always tried to do is to seek out the wisdom of those who have gone before me in life. These forerunners have such incredible wisdom, and I would be a fool not to listen. When our children were young, I remember speaking to someone about love and discipline. She said, "Never over punish for the crime; the punishment should always fit the crime." That made so much sense to me at the time. I was thinking about that statement regarding prayer and fasting. The level of prayer request or petition should probably equal the type of fast. If I am believing God to move in my life or the lives of my family in a life-changing manner, then the intensity of my prayer and fast is going to be greater than if I am fasting out of a routine.

When we were teaching our children about fasting, we talked to them about giving up something that would be a sacrifice to them and then replacing that particular thing with spending time with the Lord.

I asked my son if I could share his testimony of fasting because I believe it will make the point—fast according to the intensity of your request.

When our son, Reid, was a teenager and had begun dating, he decided that he was going to fast to meet his wife. He did not want to just keep dating and dating until he met the right one. He decided that he was going to fast and pray for his wife. He prayed before he started the fast. He asked the Lord what he should fast, and the Lord told him specifically how long to fast and what to fast. He purposed in his heart to fast for a specified amount of time and to be obedient to what the Lord had told him to fast.

He actually met his wife in December, but she was dating someone else at the time. Her relationship ended with this other young man in February. Reid's fast ended in January, and he began dating a beautiful young lady named Melissa in February. Melissa is now his wife. She is such an amazing young woman! We are so blessed to have her as a daughter! We are proud of our son and how he approached the whole process Biblically. God promised when we called out for wisdom, He would give it.

### *Praying in the Spirit*

Another type of prayer is praying in the Spirit. I like to call it my "prayer language."

**Ephesians 6:18 (NIV)**
And pray in the Spirit on all occasions with all kinds of prayers and requests. With this in mind, be alert and always keep on praying for all the Lord's people.

✧   ✧   ✧

**Jude 1:20–21 (NIV)**
But you, dear friends, by building yourselves up in
your most holy faith and praying in the Holy Spirit, [21]
keep yourselves in God's love as you wait for the mercy of our Lord Jesus Christ to bring you to eternal life.

Sometimes I will sit with the Lord, and I'm really not hearing
anything. I will begin to pray in the Spirit (in tongues). Then
my heart and mind will begin to be more in tune to His voice.
I will pray in the Spirit until I hear or see what the Lord is
saying. Once I begin to hear, I will start writing in my journal.
Now, if I've lost you there because of praying in the Spirit, just
hang in there a few more minutes.

Growing up in the church, I was never taught about
tongues—a private prayer language, if you will. All I seemed
to have ever heard about was the abuse of tongues; so personally, I had no desire to pursue it. God brought someone into
my life years ago who had such child-like faith. She always
amazed me with her level of faith for such a new believer. She
got saved in an unconventional way. No one evangelized her.
She simply said, "God, if you are real, this is what I need." She
presented her request to God, and He tangibly answered that
request. She became a Christian in that moment. So when the
Bible said it was for all men/women, she believed it.

I can remember the first time I heard someone praying in
tongues. I thought it was weird. It was very strange to me because I had not been around people who prayed like that. Yet,
I prayed and told the Lord that if it was truly from Him, then
I was interested and I wanted it.

My friend explained tongues to me very simply: When you
pray in English, you are praying from your knowledge of the
situation usually. You only have so many words or ways that

you can pray something. You also don't always know how to pray for someone. Sometimes you have no knowledge of the person or the situation. So when you receive your prayer language, you are allowing the Holy Spirit to pray through you on your behalf. Whether you are praying for your needs or someone else, the Holy Spirit knows all things, so He will know how to pray. He will pray perfectly.

Wow! That was so simple. So why wouldn't I want the Holy Spirit to pray on my behalf? I know that I can trust Him with any prayer that I have.

I noticed personally that after I had received the baptism of the Holy Spirit and I received my prayer language, that I began to see and hear more than I did before. It was different and it was wonderful!

> **Hebrews 6:1-2 (NKJV)**
> ¹ Therefore, leaving the discussion of the elementary principles of Christ, let us go on to perfection, not laying again the foundation of repentance from dead works and of faith toward God, ² of the doctrine of baptisms, of laying on of hands, of resurrection of the dead, and of eternal judgment.

Notice that Hebrews 6:1-2 states that these are foundational teachings. It also uses the plural word "baptisms." All four Gospels tell us that there are two different *baptisms*. (Matthew 3:11, Mark 1:8, Luke 3:16, John 1:33)

> **Mark 1:8 (NKJV)**
> "I indeed baptized you with water, but He will baptize you with the Holy Spirit."

I encourage you to read the Word for yourself. Ask your Heavenly Father if this gift is for you. Ask Him if this gift was only for Pentecost. Ask Him if this gift is for you today.

I really do not understand how people "do life" without Jesus. I cannot imagine not talking to Him, not hearing His wisdom for my life. He is always with me, and He is always there to talk to me, especially when I am alone. When I am burdened with life and need to call on someone, He is always there for me. He is never too busy to speak with me. He is never tired of me asking Him for help. He never tires of me asking Him to show me what to do. I don't know about you, but I cannot live this life without His voice, His presence in my life. The more time I spend with Him, the more I want to be with Him. Even though life goes on, I find that when I am busy and don't have the quiet time that I like to have with Him, I miss Him. He doesn't judge or guilt me for the time that I am not with Him. He lovingly embraces me when I come to Him. He enjoys being with me. He is truly my friend.

Have you ever had a friend that you spent a lot of time with, maybe even years? Life changes and that person moves away from you. Years pass, but somehow, when you speak to the person again, it is as though time has stood still. There's no guilt of—why haven't you called, where have you been, and so on. You simply pick up where you left off, and it seems as though there has been no time lost. It's as if they have never left you at all. That is a true friend. Jesus is a true friend who sticks closer than a brother.

**Proverbs 18:24 NIV**
"One who has unreliable friends soon comes to ruin, but there is a friend who sticks closer than a brother."

There are also times in my life when I must be able to war and stand in Jesus' name. In the midst of turmoil in my life, I have to be able to hear clearly from the Lord. In those times, I must have a clear word, a clear directive from Him. I have to be able to pour my heart out to Him. I have to be able to hear what He says for my life. When I do not know what to do, I have to be able to go to Him knowing that He is my Helper, my Guide, my Comforter, and my Strong Tower. He is my Shield. He is my Protector. He is my Banner, my covering. He is everything that I need! He is El-Shaddai—my God who is more than enough. He is Jesus, King of Kings and Lord of Lords. He is my Savior and my Friend.

## *Judging*

Finally, as you begin to hear God's voice and continue to grow in this area, God will show you personal things about others. This really is privileged information for you. Ask Jesus what you are supposed to do with that information. It is not given to you so that you can judge the person, but rather, that you have compassion and pray for them. Most times, He will show you these things so that you are able to pray and intercede for that person. Be careful not to go to that person with this information—whether it's good or bad. God is trusting you with something valuable. Ask Him what He wants you to do with that information.

# *Journaling Questions*

1.  Jesus, what do You want me to know about prayer?
2.  Holy Spirit, what do You want me to know about the gift of tongues—praying in the Spirit?
3.  Jesus, when have You been prompting me to pray for someone else, and I did not recognize that You wanted me to pray for that person?
4.  Jesus, show me anywhere in my life that I have misused information that You have given to me about another person.
5.  Jesus, when You tell me something private about someone else, what do You want me to do with that information?
6.  Repent from any misuse by your hand, and forgive anyone who has spiritually abused you in this way.

# Notes

# Chapter Thirteen

# Seeing in the Spirit

**2 Kings 6:15–17 (NKJV)**
And when the servant of the man of God arose early and went out, there was an army, surrounding the city with horses and chariots. And his servant said to him, "Alas, my master! What shall we do?" [16] So he answered, "Do not fear, for those who are with us are more than those who are with them." [17] And Elisha prayed, and said, "Lord, I pray, open his eyes that he may see." Then the Lord opened the eyes of the young man, and he saw. And behold, the mountain was full of horses and chariots of fire all around Elisha.

In this story, notice that Elisha sees, but his servant did not. Elisha prayed for the servant's eyes to be opened, and they were opened. Elisha was a prophet; the servant was not a prophet. Yet God opened the servant's heart to see in the spirit realm. Sometimes we need to see in the spirit because, like the servant, our circumstances in the natural seem to be overwhelming and unattainable. Sometimes we need to see from God's perspective.

If you do not "see" in the spirit, ask the Lord to activate all of your spiritual senses. Just as we have five senses in the natural—touch, sight, taste, smell, and hearing—we also have the same senses in the spirit. We may not experience all of them, but that doesn't mean that our spiritual senses are not as real as our natural senses.

I know people who can sometimes smell different aromas from Heaven. I've known others who have literally tasted in the spirit. They have had a specific pleasant taste in their mouth while in the spirit. I know people who see angels ministering to people in worship, and others who hear the sound of angels singing. There are times that you can tangibly feel the presence of God in a room.

God created heaven and earth. Earth is the footstool of heaven. Some of the same things exist in heaven as they do on earth. So it only makes sense that we can utilize all of the same senses.

**Isaiah 66:1–2 (NKJV)**
Thus says the Lord:
"Heaven is My throne,
And earth is My footstool.
Where is the house that you will build Me?
And where is the place of My rest?
² For all those things My hand has made,
And all those things exist,"
Says the Lord.
"But on this one will I look:
On him who is poor and of a contrite spirit,
And who trembles at My word.

✧    ✧    ✧

**Matthew 6:9–10 (NKJV)**
⁹ Our Father in heaven, Hallowed be Your name.

[10] Your kingdom come. Your will be done
On earth as it is in heaven.

Matthew 6 implies that it is possible for the same things to exist in heaven and on earth at the same time.

I do not get to decide what God chooses to show me or what experience I may have with Him; however, I can choose to be with Him and experience His presence. When God is present, miraculous things happen. It's just a side effect of His presence. He is *so amazing*!

When I first began to see in the spirit, it was during prayer and intercession. At first I would see words spelled out. After a while, I began to see pictures of things, kind of like a still photo. As my walk with the Lord continued, I began seeing more. Sometimes I would see a short video of whatever God wanted me to see. Many times, I did not understand what He was showing me, so I would ask him what it meant.

This is where journaling is helpful. I would write down in my journal every detail of what I was seeing. Then I would ask the Lord what He wanted me to know. Then I would write down what He told me about what I had seen. This is the place where I would receive His revelation and wisdom. If I didn't understand what He was telling me, I would ask Him another question. I would continue to do this until I understood what He was showing me. Everything God does is for purpose; He wastes nothing. So if He is showing me something, it means something. It's up to me to find out what it means.

As you spend more time with the Lord, this will become normal for you to ask Him what He wants you to know about what He's showing you. Again, we are using sight and hearing at the same time.

I think one of the easiest ways to see is when you are in a worship setting. If you practice in your private time, you will notice that your spiritual sight will increase. What's hard for most of us initially is getting past the thought that we are see-ing something that we created or thought. That does happen sometimes. We must remember that God placed creativity and imagination within us. There are times that you cannot get the "stuff" of the day out of your mind in order to worship the Lord. That's why praise music helps. Praise takes us from the outer courts, the stress of the day, and moves us into the inner courts. It is in that place of worship that our hearts are open, and we can then begin to sense God's presence.

If you will open your heart to what God wants to show you, then He will open up another dimension of Himself that will take you to a new place with Him. It's because we are creative by nature that we are able to spiritually see. If we had no imagination, He would not have a place of creativity to flow. Sight is where God can place pictures for us to see and then give us His instruction, His guidance, and His wisdom for our life.

God is so much bigger than the box each of us has put Him in. Allow Him to remove the restraints that you've put on Him so that He can show you what He wants to speak.

My strongest sight is usually in worship and prayer. Most of the time I see with my eyes closed, but the Lord is teaching me to see with my eyes open. As with anything that we do in life, if we want to get better at it, then we must practice to obtain our goal. If I never lift a weight, how will I strengthen my muscles? It's the same with spiritual gifts. You must learn to exercise your spiritual muscles.

### Habakkuk 2:1 (NKJV)
I will stand my watch
And set myself on the rampart,
And watch to see what He will say to me,
And what I will answer when I am corrected.

Habakkuk stands and looks to see what he will hear. Number one, he's looking (sight), and number two, after he sees, he hears. He sees a picture, an image of something, and then he waits for the Lord to tell him what it means. So there are a couple of things that he does: he sees, he waits (stands), and he hears.

Once you begin to see with spiritual eyes, your spiritual sight will probably increase. You will notice that you can also see with your eyes open—maybe more like a picture, not a video, but you will see. Sometimes we see and we don't realize that we are seeing. You may be driving down the road praying for someone, and a quick flash of a picture is superimposed over the natural surroundings. You may all of a sudden have a person or situation come to your mind. God may be speaking through a quick glance.

When I realized that I was seeing with my eyes open, even though I didn't know that I was, I was so excited. How many times have you been talking to someone and you want to minister to them, but you don't know what to say. You are listening for the Holy Spirit to say something, to lead you, but you don't hear anything. Well, sometimes He is giving you a quick flash, a glance, eyes open, so that you can see what He wants you to speak. We don't want to be weird or spooky and close our eyes while we're talking to somebody. Sight is simply another way to hear God's voice.

I don't know about you, but I'm so glad that He speaks to us in so many different ways. As I learn to "tune in" to other ways of hearing God's voice; I can trust that if I miss it one way, I will hear it in another way.

Don't compare yourself with others and what they see. Embrace your journey with the Lord. He will show you all things.

### John 16:13 (KJV)
[13] Howbeit when he, the Spirit of truth, is come, he will guide you into all truth: for he shall not speak

of himself, but whatsoever he shall hear, that shall he speak: and he will shew you things to come.

⚙  ⚙  ⚙

### John 16:13 (NKJV)

13 However, when He, the Spirit of truth, has come, He will guide you into all truth; for He will not speak on His own authority, but whatever He hears He will speak, and He will tell you things to come.

Ultimately, everything we do and say should come from a place of intimacy with the Lord. Our behaviors, mindsets, and the way we treat other people should all be a reflection of our time spent in a personal relationship with God. The fruit of the Holy Spirit should be an overflow of our lives with Christ.

### Galatians 5:22-23 (NKJV)

22 But the fruit of the Spirit is love, joy, peace, long-suffering, kindness, goodness, faithfulness, 23 gentleness, self-control. Against such there is no law.

As we learn to hear God's voice in the quiet; we will then be able to hear and recognize His voice when there is noise all around. Take time to practice hearing Him when there's no one around, such as when the electronics are turned off. It's in the training ground of your private time with the Lord that will enable you to be sensitive to His voice in the midst of noise. We want to hear Him everywhere we go. We want to walk, knowing that we are a conduit for the Holy Spirit to move through at any moment.

### Isaiah 60:2 (NKJV)

2 For behold, the darkness shall cover the earth,
And deep darkness the people;

But the Lord will arise over you,
And His glory will be seen upon you.

That is why: we are the hope for the lost. We are Jesus' light in a world of darkness. Let us hear, speak, and move in harmony with the Holy Spirit.

# *Journaling Questions and Exercises*

1. Lord, with all of the new-age teaching everywhere, what do You want me to know about seeing in the Spirit?
2. Lord, is it okay to see in the Spirit?
3. Ask the Lord to activate all of your spiritual senses.
4. Put on some worship music. Love on the Lord for a while. Close your natural eyes and look to see what He will speak to you.
5. Lord, show me a picture of something about me. Write down what you saw regardless of how short or how long it was. Then ask the Lord what He wants you to know about those pictures or images you saw.
6. Lord, what else do You want me to know today?

# Notes

# Chapter Fourteen

# Dreams

God loves to speak to us in many ways. Dreams are another way that He speaks to us.

### 1 Kings 3:3–15 (NKJV)

³ And Solomon loved the Lord, walking in the statutes of his father David, except that he sacrificed and burned incense at the high places.
⁴ Now the king went to Gibeon to sacrifice there, for that was the great high place: Solomon offered a thousand burnt offerings on that altar. ⁵ At Gibeon the Lord appeared to Solomon in a dream by night, and God said, "Ask! What shall I give you?"
⁶ And Solomon said: "You have shown great mercy to Your servant David my father, because he walked before You in truth, in righteousness, and in uprightness of heart with You; You have continued this great kindness for him, and You have given him a son to sit on his throne, as it is this day. ⁷ Now, O Lord my God, You have made Your servant king instead of my father David, but I am

a little child; I do not know how to go out or come in. ⁸ And Your servant is in the midst of Your people whom You have chosen, a great people, too numerous to be numbered or counted. ⁹ Therefore give to Your servant an understanding heart to judge Your people, that I may discern between good and evil. For who is able to judge this great people of Yours?"

¹⁰ The speech pleased the Lord, that Solomon had asked this thing. ¹¹ Then God said to him: "Because you have asked this thing, and have not asked long life for yourself, nor have asked riches for yourself, nor have asked the life of your enemies, but have asked for yourself understanding to discern justice, ¹² behold, I have done according to your words; see, I have given you a wise and understanding heart, so that there has not been anyone like you before you, nor shall any like you arise after you. ¹³ And I have also given you what you have not asked: both riches and honor, so that there shall not be anyone like you among the kings all your days. ¹⁴ So if you walk in My ways, to keep My statutes and My commandments, as your father David walked, then I will lengthen your days."

¹⁵ Then Solomon awoke, and indeed it had been a dream. And he came to Jerusalem and stood before the ark of the covenant of the Lord, offered up burnt offerings, offered peace offerings, and made a feast for all his servants.

✧ ✧ ✧

**1 Kings 3:28 (NLT)**

²⁸ When all Israel heard the king's decision, the people were in awe of the king, for they saw the wisdom God had given him for rendering justice.

Think about this amazing story of Solomon. God spoke to Solomon in a dream saying, "Ask for whatever you want Me to give you." Solomon responds in verse 9: "Therefore give to Your servant an understanding heart to judge Your people, that I may discern between good and evil. For who is able to judge this great people of Yours."

In 1 Kings 3:10 Then God said to him:

> Because you have asked this thing, and have not asked long life for yourself, nor have asked riches for yourself, nor have asked the life of your enemies, but have asked for yourself understanding to discern justice, ¹² behold, I have done according to your words; see, I have given you a wise and understanding heart, so that there has not been anyone like you, before you, nor shall any like you arise after you.

In verse ¹⁵ it says that Solomon awoke and indeed it had been a dream. Wow! What a conversation, and a two-way one at that! Solomon received so much. Do you realize that Solomon was sleeping and he was talking to God? His body was asleep but his spirit was having a talk with God Almighty. Wow!

In verses 16–27, this was confirmed by the first decision he made in front of the people. In verse 28 it says, All of Israel saw that the wisdom of God was in him.

A friend of mine used to say that she would wake up in the morning, and she would just know things. It didn't really make sense to me at the time. When you read the story of

Solomon and realize what was taking place, you can now understand that he was talking to God in the night. So, for those of you who wake up in the morning, and you "just know" stuff about the Lord, His Kingdom, an answer to your prayer, and so forth, maybe your spirit has been talking to God while you were sleeping, and that's how "you know."

### Job 33:14-18 (NKJV)

[14] For God may speak in one way, or in another, Yet man does not perceive it. [15] In a dream, in a vision of the night, When deep sleep falls upon men, While slumbering on their beds, [16] Then He opens the ears of men, And seals their instruction. [17] In order to turn man from his deed, And conceal pride from man, [18] He keeps back his soul from the Pit, And his life from perishing by the sword.

Joseph, the most well-known dreamer in the Bible, was able to save a nation because of the dreams that God had given him. He didn't know what they meant when he was young, but God later confirmed his early dreams to him through his life. God spoke to Joseph through a dream which when interpreted foretold his future and the future of Israel. Some dreams are for the present and some are for our future. Here is the dream and the fulfillment:

### Genesis 37:5–11 (NKJV)

[5] Now Joseph had a dream, and he told it to his brothers, and they hated him even more. [6] So he said to them, "Please hear this dream which I have dreamed: [7] There we were, binding sheaves in the field. Then behold, my sheaf arose and also stood upright, and indeed your sheaves stood all around and bowed down to my sheaf." [8] And his brothers said to him, "Shall you indeed reign over us?

Or shall you indeed have dominion over us?" So they hated him even more for his dreams and for his words. ⁹ Then he dreamed still another dream and told it to his brothers, and said, "Look, I have dreamed another dream. And this time, the sun, the moon, and the eleven stars bowed down to me." ¹⁰ So he told it to his father and his brothers, and his father rebuked him and said to him, "What is this dream that you have dreamed? Shall your mother and I and your brothers indeed come to bow down to the earth before you?" ¹ And his brothers envied him, but his father kept the matter in mind.

✧   ✧   ✧

**Genesis 45:4–8 (NKJV)**
⁴ And Joseph said to his brothers, "Please come near to me." So they came near. Then he said: "I am Joseph your brother, whom you sold into Egypt. ⁵ But now, do not therefore be grieved or angry with yourselves because you sold me here; for God sent me before you to preserve life. ⁶ For these two years the famine has been in the land, and there are still five years in which there will be neither plowing nor harvesting. ⁷ And God sent me before you to preserve a posterity for you in the earth, and to save your lives by a great deliverance. ⁸ So now it was not you who sent me here, but God, and He has made me a father to Pharaoh, and lord of all his house, and a ruler throughout all the land of Egypt.

If you're in a season of dreaming, write down your dreams in as much detail as you can remember. Make note of how you are feeling in the dream—fearful, angry, peaceful, and so on. Also make note of colors, names, and places. The wisdom and truth of a dream can be powerful. Don't disregard your dreams, especially if it stays with you through the day. You may think that you will remember it all later, but more than likely, you will not remember the dream. Some dreams stand out, and you will remember every detail for days. Usually, as your day gets going, details will begin to fade. So it's a good practice to keep a notebook by your bed. When you awake from your dream, write it down in as much detail as possible.

There are many great books on dream language. Make sure that the authors are Christ-centered believers. There is a lot of new-age teaching on dreams, so be careful when choosing these books. James Goll, Perry Stone, John Paul Jackson, and many others have great books that teach on dream interpretation.

Most people dream symbolically rather than literally. If you dream literally, it will come true just as you saw it in the dream. People that dream literally usually have fewer dreams or don't remember many dreams, but when they have them, they know that they are significant. As I said before, most of us dream symbolically and each of us has our own dream symbolism. So when you're interpreting your dream, the people in the dream will represent someone else or something else. Sometimes it's hard to separate the symbolism from life, but ask the Lord to make the interpretation clear to you.

I've had dreams that have been warnings from the Lord. I remember one in particular where the Lord warned me to not respond in the flesh in the same way that I had responded in the dream. Within two weeks of the dream, a situation came up identical to the dream. As I was standing in the situation, God reminded me of the dream, and because of it, I knew how I was supposed to respond.

When our boys were younger and they would dream, I remember how the symbolism in their dreams was so much different than ours. One son used to have dreams about gaming characters, gaming strategies, and solutions. One dreamed about school and other students. That's where they were in life, so God spoke to them in a way that they would understand. God uses the things in each of our lives to speak to us. If you love boating, you'll probably have dreams relating to the ocean or nautical things, such as sea life. God does not do everything one way. He is constantly speaking, and He loves for us to pursue Him to hear what He has to say.

As we've discussed in previous chapters, we must learn how to hear God's voice by exercising different means to hear Him. There are two different types of dreams that I'm going to talk about which I call "Fear Dreams." There are dreams that are from the enemy that are tormenting which cause fear. When you recognize that it's from the enemy, disregard it. There are also dreams about fear that are from the Lord.

Here's a key: The enemy comes to steal (your peace), kill, and destroy, but Jesus comes to give life in abundance.

There have been times when I woke up from a dream, and I was breathing very hard, shaking or trying to catch my breath. Those were not dreams from the Lord. When you wake up and you are afraid, it's most likely from the enemy.

The Lord will sometimes show you your fears in a dream so that He can bring healing to you. God's heart is always about helping us, making us better, and restoring us. His heart is not to harm us but to heal us. Dreams will show us emotional fears that we may have. So if the Lord shows you a specific fear in a dream, journal about it. It's not to make you fearful; it's to make you healthy. Ask Him for His wisdom and His truth about the dream.

# *Journaling Questions*

1.  Why do You speak through dreams?
2.  Lord, what do You want me to know about the dreams that I dream at night?
3.  Lord, please give me a dream tonight. When I wake up, help me to remember the dream and make it plain to me that it's from You—and then give me the interpretation.

# Notes

# Chapter Fifteen

# Worship

I couldn't close this book without talking about worship. There is a correlation between hearing God's voice and worship. Worship is so intimate to me. It is a place where I am with the Lord and totally untouched by the outside world.

I accepted Christ at the age of fourteen, but I walked away from Him for three and a half years. During that time, I would go out and party with friends only to come home and feel totally empty inside. When I was out in the world, one of my favorite things to do was to go dancing. For me, when I was dancing, there was a feeling that I was safe from the world, and no one could get to me there in that place. It was an emotional as well as physical high. I loved being in that place.

When I rededicated my life to the Lord, for weeks after that, I would still go out dancing—not partying, just dancing. I didn't have a problem with dancing. When I gave my heart to the Lord, He took away every desire for drugs or alcohol, yet I still desired to dance. I still dance, but it's for an audience of one—Jesus.

One evening as I was heading out for the night, I heard the Lord speak. It may as well have been audible because it was so clear. He asked: "Would you be willing to give it all up for

Me? If you do, I will give you something far greater in return."
I really didn't understand the depth of what He meant at the
time; I simply understood that He had something better for
me than going out barhopping.

For the next seven or eight years, the Lord was teaching me
so many things. I served where I felt the Lord calling me to
serve at the time—the church choir. I loved to sing; so I was a
part of the music ministry for a number of years. The Lord was
giving me glimpses of worship. We had a few different worship leaders during that time, and you could sense something
different in worship. It was not about singing songs to fill a
service; it was about bringing love to the Lord through worship in song. I could sense a stirring within me, but I didn't
really know what it was.

A few years later, I had an experience with God in worship
that I had never had before. In that setting of worship, God
stirred something so deep within me that I would never be the
same again. It seemed as if I could tangibly feel His presence.
This was new to me. There was such an overwhelming feeling
of love and peace in the room. That's the best way that I can
describe what I felt at the time. What I knew in that moment
was that I could never go back to the way that I worshipped
Him, the way that I pursued Him. God placed a longing in me
to be with Him that nothing else or no one else can fill. I now
understand what He wanted to exchange in my life, and I am
so grateful that He wants to be with me. I love Him so much!
I look forward to every encounter with Him. He is *amazing*!

What God gave me in exchange was a lifestyle of worship
and knowing Him. As I laid down my stuff and came before
Him and loved on Him in worship, He gave me something
greater—Himself—His presence. There was and is no greater
high than being in the Lord's presence. There was no safer
place than being in His presence. What I gave up was so small

compared to the greatness of who He is. When I worship, I choose to not be a spectator. I choose to exalt the One who died for me. Jesus saved me from a life of loneliness, a life filled with fear and self-destruction.

Worship is a big part of our lives. I believe it to be a very important aspect of the Christian life. There's something that takes place during Spirit-led worship that changes us. When you surrender your soul in worship, there is an exchange. The lists of prayer requests seem to subside after you have been in the presence of the King. It's not that our needs are not important because they are; it's just that after being with Him, you have a new confidence that He is working on the things in your life. When I walk away from a worship setting, in the natural my problems or needs have not changed; however, my perspective and my peace are different. I walk away from the Lord being encouraged. Hope for my situation has changed.

Worship is an essential part of a Christian's walk; it's not just an option, in my opinion. Worship is a lifestyle, and it will forever change you if you will allow it. Worship is about loving our Father. It's about loving Jesus. It's about loving the Holy Spirit. Worship is freely giving love to the Creator. Worshipping the Lord through music is just one of the many ways to worship.

Worship is also a key for many to help them hear the voice of God. Many people find that after being in the presence of God, it is so much easier to hear His voice. If you engage in worship, the things of this world will fade away, and you will be left standing before the King. As a practical tool, keep a journal with you when you go into a worship setting. As the Holy Spirit begins speaking or talking to you, write down what you are hearing.

We have home groups in our church that we call Life Groups. In our Life Group, we usually study a particular topic, and

then we have a time of worship. When the music stops, we
don't jump up and start moving around. The presence of God
is so sweet. This is a perfect time for people to just wait on
Him and sit in His presence. It's in these moments that many
people find it easier to hear from Him. At this point, we will
journal as to what the Lord is speaking to us. The problems
and cares of the day have faded from our minds. Our focus is
on Jesus. Life situations may not have changed in the natural,
but things are changing in the Spirit. Hope is restored. God is
changing each of us in His presence. He is so amazing!

I would like to end this book with worship. Keep your journal close by so that you can write down what the Lord shows
you or speaks to you. Take time to just wait on Him. Worship
Him and He will show up. He inhabits the praises of His people. He hangs out where His people worship Him. He loves to
hear your voice. He loves to be with you.

**Psalms 22:3 (NKJV)**
But You are holy,
Enthroned in the praises of Israel.

&#9674;   &#9674;   &#9674;

**Acts 16:25 (NKJV)**
But at midnight Paul and Silas were praying and
singing hymns to God, and the prisoners were listening to them. [26] Suddenly there was a great earth-
quake, so that the foundations of the prison were
shaken, and immediately all the doors were opened
and everyone's chains were loosed.

I want to encourage you right now to put on some music
and pursue God in worship. Don't go in with an agenda. Don't
go in expecting only to receive from Him. Worship the Lord

with all that you are and all that you have. I promise you, there will be an exchange.

As I was worshipping one day, the Lord gave me these words. I thought they were just for me, but He said that they were for *you*.

Excerpt from the Lord:

> "I love that you've come to worship Me. I love that you have brought a new song to Me. I love to hear you sing. I love to hear your praises. I love to be with you. I love when you pour out your heart to Me with such passion. I love to hear your voice. I love everything about you. I love you!"

### End Note

[1] Don and Katie Fortune. 1989. *Discover your Children's Gifts.* Old Tappan, New Jersey: Chosen Books.